Comprehensive Reading: Getting Key Skills through 15 Topics

読解力を磨く現代の話題 15 章

by
Tom Dillon
Michael Schauerte
Koji Nishiya

TSURUMI SHOTEN

画像クレジット一覧

Unit 1　©Jürgen Fälchle–fotolia.com
Unit 2　©Brocreative–fotolia.com
Unit 3　©vetre–fotolia.com
Unit 4　©trueblackheart–fotolia.com
Unit 5　©Photographee.eu–fotolia.com
Unit 6　©AntonioDiaz–fotolia.com
Unit 7　©sonyakamoz–fotolia.com
Unit 8　©denisismagilov–fotolia.com
Unit 9　©aletia2011–fotolia.com
Unit 10　©divedog–fotolia.com
Unit 11　©mokee81–fotolia.com
Unit 12　©auremar–fotolia.com
Unit 13　©rook76–fotolia.com
Unit 14　©pillerss–fotolia.com
Unit 15　©Sebastiano Fancellu–fotolia.com
表紙　　©ra2 studio–fotolia.com

はしがき

　私たちは今、インターネットをとおして世界中の情報にアクセスできます。その情報は個人が発信したもの、団体や企業が発信したものだったり、媒体もブログ、Facebook、Twitter、ホームページなど、じつに様々です。ひと昔前なら、図書館などで文献に当たって手間暇かけて手に入れていた情報が大量に、また、簡単に手に入ります。

　しかし、人が情報を読み取って理解する作業は、昔とあまり変わりません。ですから、効率の良い情報の処理の仕方（＝読み方）をしなければ、大量の情報の海に溺れて、読むことが苦行になってしまいます。逆に、効率よく読むことができれば、昔の出来事や、他の人の思い、考え、また、今起きていることなど、これまで知らなかったことをますます知ることができるようになり、読むこと自体が楽しいと思えるようになってきます。

　本書は、この読むことの楽しさを体験できるようになるために、様ざまなテーマの英文を400語程度のパッセージにまとめました。健康、旅行、ペットなどの身近なテーマから、歴史、社会学、伝記などの少し固いテーマが、15ユニットにちりばめられています。各ユニットには豊富なトレーニングを取り入れました。パッセージを構成するパラグラフの構造を捉えるトレーニングを中心に、Comprehension Questions、内容要約、さらに、英作文をとおして、効率よく読むスキルが身につき、読む楽しさが実感できるように工夫してあります。

　本書を執筆するにあたり、豊富なジャンルからいろいろなトピックの英文を作成していただいたマイケル・シャワティー氏・トム・ディロン氏にあらためて心からお礼申し上げます。

　本書を通じて、英文を読む楽しさを体験し、世界とのつながりが豊かになることの一助になれば、著者としても大きな喜びです。

2016年11月

著者代表　西谷　恒志

CONTENTS

Unit 1	**Science/Technology**	○宇宙船の副産物○	
	From Outer Space, To Your Space		1
Unit 2	**Sports**	○フットボール人気の陰で○	
	Injuries Hurt Football's Popularity		6
Unit 3	**Health**	○断食の功罪○	
	Gaining Popularity Fast		11
Unit 4	**History**	○カナダのゴールドラッシュ○	
	The Klondike Gold Rush		16
Unit 5	**Psychology**	○内気のすばらしさ○	
	Are You Shy?		21
Unit 6	**Animals**	○アメリカのペット・ビジネス○	
	Pet Profits		26
Unit 7	**Food**	○地中海式ダイエット○	
	Eating the Mediterranean Way		31
Unit 8	**Art**	○芸術のハブ都市ニューヨーク○	
	New York as Artistic Hub		36
Unit 9	**Biography**	○世紀の大悪党ジョン・デリンジャー○	
	John Dillinger—Public Enemy No. 1		41
Unit 10	**Tourism**	○ハワイの隠れた名所○	
	The Attraction of Kealakekua Bay		46
Unit 11	**Social Problem**	○卑劣なネットいじめ○	
	Cyber-Bullying		51
Unit 12	**Language**	○通訳者の能力とは○	
	A Job for Fast Talkers and Fast Thinkers		56
Unit 13	**Literature**	○小説はどこに○	
	Graphic Novels		61
Unit 14	**Culture**	○アムステルダム風景○	
	Canal Houses		66
Unit 15	**Sociology**	○運転中にナゼキレる?○	
	Road Rage		71

各ユニットの構成

■ 豊富なジャンルとトピック
15 ユニットの中に、豊富なジャンルとトピックの英文が入っています。

★ タイトル
タイトルは本文の内容に密接に関連した語句や、内容を数語で凝縮した語句でできています。

★ 英文
豊富なジャンルから様ざまなトピックを選びました。
第1パラグラフには、多くの場合、本文の主題文（トピックセンテンス）が入っています。

★ Keywords & Keyphrases
キーとなる単語・熟語：マッチングの問題形式。

★ Exercises 1
英文の構成理解。ディスコース・マーカー中心に。
論理関係、時間などを示す重要な語句が入る適切な箇所を問う問題です。問題を解くことで、パッセージを構成するパラグラフ間の関係や、論理の流れが理解できます。

★ Exercises 2
Comprehension Questions: 2 問
パッセージの内容に関して、全体的なことを問う質問と、具体的な情報を問う質問です。

★ Exercises 3
True-False: 3 問
パッセージの内容に一致しているかどうかを問う問題です。

★ Exercises 4
内容要約文完成と空所補充問題
空所に語句を入れて、パッセージの要約文を完成させる問題です。

★ Exercises 5
部分英作文
パッセージに出てくる語句をターゲットにした問題。授業では音声を利用したディクテーション問題にもなります。

Unit 1 Science/Technology

宇宙船の副産物

From Outer Space, To Your Space

NASA（アメリカ航空宇宙局）は1958年の設立以来、アポロ11号による史上初で唯一の月面着陸をはじめ、スペースシャトル、国際宇宙ステーション(ISS)、ハッブル宇宙望遠鏡など、数々の偉業を成し遂げてきているが、一方で、毎年巨大な予算を費やしており、最近では、毎年約1900億ドル（約2兆円）の予算となっている。一部にはこれを無駄な予算との批判もあるが、これまでの宇宙開発計画により数多くの発見・発明がなされてきたことも事実である。

　The American space program led by the National Aeronautics* and Space Administration (NASA) has resulted in many amazing accomplishments. Most people focus on such feats as the first trip to the moon or the unmanned missions to explore planets in our solar system. But there are many other benefits to our everyday lives that have resulted from the space program.

　Ever since NASA was created in 1958, the Administration has been involved in transferring its technologies for use in other fields. The term "spinoff" was created to describe how NASA technologies are transferred for other uses. (　A　), NASA has achieved over 1,500 spinoffs that have benefited human beings.

　Some of these technologies might have been developed eventually, but there

UNIT 1　Science/Technology

is no question that the space program helped to speed up the pace of innovation. Despite the amazing success of NASA in creating innovative new technologies, however, the Administration has not done a very good job of making the public aware of these achievements. In fact, some people wonder if it is worthwhile for the United States to spend so much money on its space program.

But if we take a brief look at some of the technologies that have emerged thanks to NASA research in such fields as physics, engineering, biology, and medicine, it becomes clear that the space program is worthwhile.

(　B　), for example, NASA developed a new type of fabric for the spacesuits* of astronauts made from Teflon-coated fiberglass*. This same material was later used as a material to create roofs for buildings and stadiums. The technology used to create the spacesuits astronauts wore on the moon, which had used a liquid-cooled system to resist high temperatures, was also used later as a way to treat physical injuries.

There have also been numerous medical benefits resulting from NASA technologies. In 1994, a company in the United States developed a mechanical arm that doctors can use to operate on patients based on the technologies that NASA had used to repair spacecraft. (　C　), an artificial heart pump was invented by Dr. Michael DeBakey* and engineer David Saucier*. This heart pump was designed on the basis of the main engine fuel pumps of NASA's space shuttle.

These are just a few of the many examples of the practical benefits on Earth from the exploration of space in the past few decades.　　　　(398 words)

*Aeronautics [eərənɔ́ːtics]「航空学」　*spacesuits「宇宙服」　*fiberglass「グラスファイバー、繊維ガラス」　*Dr. Michael DeBakey　マイケル・ドベイキー博士。アメリカの著名な心臓外科医。
*David Saucier　デイヴィッド・ソーシエ。NASAのエンジン部門の技術者。心筋梗塞でドベイキー博士による心臓移植手術を1984年に受けた。1996年に死去。

Keywords & Keypharases

本文に使われている次の語句の意味として最も適切なものをa~jから選びなさい。

1. (l. 3)　focus on　　　　a. 偉業、手柄　　　　　　1. (　　)
2. (l. 3)　feat　　　　　　b. 副産物、副次効果　　　2. (　　)
3. (l. 3)　unmanned　　　 c. 宇宙船　　　　　　　　3. (　　)
4. (l. 7)　transfer　　　　 d. 織物、生地　　　　　　4. (　　)
5. (l. 7)　spinoff　　　　　e. 出現する、現れる　　　5. (　　)

6.	(l. 16) emerge	f.	に耐える、に抵抗する	6. (	)
7.	(l. 19) fabric	g.	を移植する、を移動する	7. (	)
8.	(l. 23) liquid-cooled	h.	に焦点を当てる、に注目する	8. (	)
9.	(l. 23) resist	i.	液冷 (式) の	9. (	)
10.	(l. 28) spacecraft	j.	無人の	10. (	)

Exercises

1 本文中の空欄 (A), (B), (C) に入る単語として最も適切なものをそれぞれ①〜③の中から選びなさい。

(A) ....
(B) ....
(C) ....

① Back in the 1970s
② Up to now
③ Around that same time

2 質問を読み、正しい答を (A) 〜 (D) の中から選びなさい。

Question 1

What is the main topic of this passage?

(A) The need to further expand the space program
(B) The successful businesses operated by NASA
(C) NASA moon missions' impact on technologies
(D) Useful technologies arising from the space program

Question 2

What happened in the 1994, according to the passage?

(A) NASA began to study the numerous medical benefits of its technologies.
(B) A medical device was developed based on the engine fuel pump.
(C) A mechanical arm was developed by astronauts to repair the space shuttle.
(D) Patients were operated on using an artificial heart pump designed by NASA.

UNIT 1   Science/Technology

3 次の英文は本文の内容に関するものである。本文の内容に一致する場合は T を、一致しない場合は F を下線部に記入しなさい。

(A) NASA has always transferred technologies to other fields.　　..................

(B) Some wonder if the United States should spend so much money on its PR.
　　..................

(C) A fabric developed by NASA was later used as a building material.
　　..................

4 次は本文の要約文である。空欄（ A ）（ B ）（ C ）に入れるべき適切なものをそれぞれ①〜③から選んで要約文を完成させなさい。

The space program in the United States has led to many amazing achievements, (A) the famous mission to the moon. (B) equally impressive are the numerous technologies that have emerged from the space program to help improve our daily lives. (C) there are many examples of technologies that have been used in such fields as engineering and medicine, NASA needs to do a better job of publicizing the benefits of its technologies.

* publicize を宣伝する

(A) ....　［① including　② seeing　③ starting］

(B) ....　［① And　② But　③ Then］

(C) ....　［① Until　② Though　③ If］

5 空所に入れる最も適切な語句を選択肢 (A) ～ (C) から選びなさい。

(1) 訓練初日には、チーム・スキルを構築することに焦点を当てる。

For the first day of training, we will (　　) building team skills.

(A) focus on　　　(B) serve on　　　(C) bring on

(1) ....

(2) 昼夜飲まず食わずで 74 日間断食することは、信じられない偉業である。

Fasting for seventy-four days and nights without eating or drinking is an incredible (　　).

(A) feat　　　(B) ritual　　　(C) impulse

(2) ....

(3) 国内の銀行口座へ振り込むのにいくらかかりますか？

How much does it cost to (　　) money to other domestic bank accounts?

(A) grant　　　(B) withdraw　　　(C) transfer

(3) ....

(4) その車は脇道から突然現れ、道を渡っていた男性を驚かせた。

The car suddenly (　　) from a side street and surprised the man crossing the street.

(A) departed　　　(B) erupted　　　(C) emerged

(4) ....

(5) 新しい考えに抵抗を示す人がいるが、それは提案をした人に用心しているからだ。

Some people (　　) new ideas because they are cautious of the person making the proposal.

(A) regulate　　　(B) resist　　　(C) resort

(5) ....

Unit 2　Sports

フットボール人気の陰で

Injuries Hurt Football's Popularity

アメリカで最も人気のあるスポーツはフットボールであり、2位以下の野球やバスケットボールを大きく引き離している。中でもNFLは北米プロスポーツリーグで最も人気があり、そのチャンピオンシップを決めるスーパーボールは全米で1億人以上がテレビ観戦をするほどである。一方で近年、フットボールをする子どもを持つ親たちのあいだでは、安全に対する関心が高まっている。こうした背景のもと、安全に対するNFLの取り組みと成果、今後の課題などに触れる。

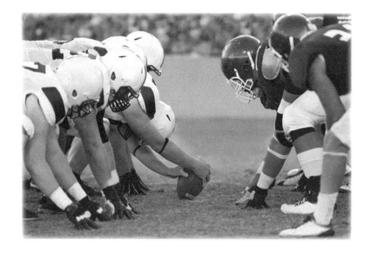

　　Football* is one of the most popular sports in the United States. Every year, more than 110 million Americans watch the Super Bowl* (the championship of the National Football League) on TV. Many children enjoy playing football outside with their friends or on their junior- or senior-high school teams. (　A　) more and more parents are worrying about the health risks of playing this very physical sport. In particular, parents are concerned about the large number of head injuries, such as concussions, that occur among football players.

　　The National Football League, or NFL, has been trying to reduce the number of injuries among its players by changing some of the game's rules and improving the safety of the helmets that players wear. These efforts seem to have borne some fruit. In 2014, for example, the number of concussions suffered by players decreased by 25% compared to the previous year, according to the NFL.

But such improvements have not been enough to convince some parents that the game is safe for their children to play. The widespread concern about head injuries has resulted in fewer children playing football in the United States. In fact, according to one survey, the number of kids playing in youth football leagues fell by nearly 10% in the period from 2010 to 2012.

Along with the danger of head injuries, there are even a number of deaths every year related to football games. According to the National Center for Catastrophic Sport Injury Research*, there were 17 deaths either directly or indirectly related to playing football among high-school players in 2013. (B   ) this statistic is worrying, it is worth remembering that around 1.1 million high-school students played football that year, so the cases of death are quite rare.

Other parents think that the health risks of football are exaggerated and that the dangers of other sports are overlooked. They argue that there is always some risk in the case of any kind of physical activity. Such parents believe that football has received the brunt of criticism, (C   ) other relatively dangerous sports —like gymnastics or horseback riding—have not been subject to such scrutiny.

Although there is much disagreement about how dangerous it is to play football, there is a basic consensus that efforts should be undertaken to make the game as safe as possible. Both professional and amateur football teams now realize that the sport will have no future unless its safety can be improved.

(409 words)

*football　アメリカでは主にアメリカンフットボール、イギリスでは主にサッカーを指す。
*Super Bowl「スーパーボウル」(＊アメリカのプロアメリカンフットボール(NFL)の優勝決定戦。アメリカ最大のスポーツイベント。) *National Center for Catastrophic Sport Injury Research「重度スポーツ障害研究ナショナルセンター」

Keywords & Keyphrases

本文に使われている次の語句の意味としてもっとも適切なものをa~jから選びなさい。

1. (l.7) injury   a. 矢面、矛先   1. (   )
2. (l.7) concussion   b. けが、傷害   2. (   )
3. (ll.19-) catastrophic c. 監視；精密な調査   3. (   )
4. (l.22) statistic   d. 脳しんとう   4. (   )
5. (l.24) exaggerate   e. 統計値、統計量   5. (   )

UNIT 2　Sports

6. (l. 25)　overlook　　　　f. を誇張する、を強調する　　6. (　　)
7. (l. 27)　brunt　　　　　g. に取り掛かる；を引き受ける　7. (　　)
8. (l. 28)　subject to　　　h. を見逃す；を見晴らす　　　8. (　　)
9. (l. 28)　scrutiny　　　　i. を受けやすい、にかかりやすい　9. (　　)
10. (l. 30)　undertake　　　j. 致命的な、壊滅的な　　　　10. (　　)

Exercises

1 本文中の空欄（ A),(B),(C ）に入る単語として最も適切なものをそれぞれ①、②の中から選びなさい。

(A)　..................................
(B)　..................................
(C)　..................................

(A)	① And	② But
(B)	① Although	② Because
(C)	① Because	② While

2 質問を読み、正しい答を (A) ～ (D) の中から選びなさい。

Question 1

What is the main point of this article?

(A) Football is the most dangerous sport in the world.
(B) Most parents think the risks of football are exaggerated.
(C) There is an increasing debate about the safety of football.
(D) People are no longer interested in watching football games on TV.

Question 2

What has the NFL been trying to do?

(A) To improve the safety of the football audience
(B) To encourage players to wear helmets
(C) To track the number of players' concussions
(D) To bring down the number of player injuries

3 次の英文は本文の内容に関するものである。本文の内容に一致する場合はTを、一致しない場合はFを下線部に記入しなさい。

(A) Injuries in youth football leagues fell by nearly 10% from 2010 to 2012.

....

(B) There are very few deaths resulting from football among high-school students.

....

(C) More and more parents are worried about the dangers of gymnastics and horse-back riding.

....

4 次は本文の要約文である。空欄（ A),(B),(C),(D ）に入れるべき適切なものをそれぞれ①、②から選んで要約文を完成させなさい。

Football remains a popular sport in the United States, but in recent years more and more parents are worried about the safety of the sport. (A) these concerns, the number of children playing on football teams has (B). (C) parents think the dangers of football are exaggerated, (D) in general people are calling for the sport to be made safer.

(A) .... [① Because of   ② Inspite of]

(B) .... [① increased   ② decreased]

(C) .... [① Some   ② Many]

(D) .... [① so   ② but]

UNIT 2　Sports

5　空所に入れる最も適切な語句を選択肢 (A) 〜 (C) から選びなさい。

(1) 飲み始めたときにどのような気分であっても、アルコールによってしばしば誇張される。

　　Alcohol will often (　　) whatever mood you're in when you start drinking.

　　　(A) transform　　　(B) modify　　　(C) exaggerate

　　　　　　　　　　　　　　　　　　　　　　　　(1) ....

(2) 不幸なことに警察はその犯人が隠れていた一つの部屋を見逃した。

　　Unfornunately the police (　　) the one room in which the criminal hid.

　　　(A) overlooked　　　(B) overtook　　　(C) overcame

　　　　　　　　　　　　　　　　　　　　　　　　(2) ....

(3) 出かける日の朝にご確認ください。公園の開園時間は変わりやすいからです。

　　Please check back on the morning of the day you are going to visit, because park hours are (　　) change.

　　　(A) relevant to　　　(B) subject to　　　(C) welcome to

　　　　　　　　　　　　　　　　　　　　　　　　(3) ....

(4) 報道によれば、自動車メーカーに対する規制当局の監視は世界的に増大している。

　　The media reports regulatory (　　) on automakers is rising globally.

　　　(A) scrutiny　　　(B) struggle　　　(C) scheme

　　　　　　　　　　　　　　　　　　　　　　　　(4) ....

(5) 私は修士課程を卒業する前に、研究課題に着手しなければならない。

　　I have to (　　) a research project before I can graduate from my master's course.

　　　(A) overwhelm　　　(B) perform　　　(C) undertake

　　　　　　　　　　　　　　　　　　　　　　　　(5) ....

Unit 3 Health

断食の功罪

Gaining Popularity Fast

断食 (Fasting) は古来よりいろいろな宗教で行われている。イスラム教ではラマダンの期間中には断食が行われる。一方、アメリカでは宗教に関係なく、健康志向の人のあいだで支持を得ており、減量目的で断食が行われている。だが、医者の中には、断食終了後のリバウンドや、健康的に食べたり運動したりすることに対する関心の低下をデメリットにあげる者もいる。つまり、健康目的の断食には賛否両論があり、本当にヘルシーかどうかについては、まだ不明という。

　Recently, in the United States and elsewhere, there is a growing trend toward "fasting" — in other words, skipping a meal (　A　) even not eating for an entire day. The custom in the past was often connected to a particular religion, such as the Muslim* custom of Ramadan*. But these days people are opting to fast for perceived health reasons, claiming that there are numerous benefits from fasting on a regular basis.

　So what are the arguments in favor of fasting? The obvious reason for some people is simply as an expedient way to lose weight. Cutting out a meal every few days obviously reduces calorie intake, which can lead to weight loss. But there are other apparent benefits of cutting back on the amount of food we eat by

UNIT 3　Health

regularly skipping a meal. Some have claimed that this can reduce the level of cholesterol or lower blood pressure. And others have said that fasting can help prevent diabetes.

There seems to be some scientific basis regarding the benefits of fasting, at least with regard to weight loss. One reason is that after a person has not eaten for around 8 hours, the body begins to use up the glucose that has been stored — (　B　) after that the body begins to burn the stored fat, resulting in weight loss.

But there are also risks associated with regular fasting. One of the biggest dangers is dehydration resulting from the body not having access to the fluid from food that it usually absorbs. Some people who fast have complained about such side effects as headaches or lack of sleep. It is also not uncommon for a person to have a stomachache because thinking about food or smelling it can result in the stomach producing acid in preparation for a meal (that does not arrive).

Some doctors even question whether fasting is an effective weight-loss method. Certainly, fasting is a way to lose weight quickly, (　C　) many people seem to gain the weight back just as quickly once they start eating regular meals again. There is also the danger that people will view fasting as the key solution, and end up paying less attention to the importance of eating healthy meals and exercising.

The fasting boom has opened up a rigorous debate over its pros and cons — and so it is not clear yet whether this trend is healthy or not.　(395 words)

Muslim [mʌ́zləm, múz-, mús-]「イスラム教徒、イスラム教（徒）の」 *Ramadan* [ræmədɑ́ːn]「ラマダーン、断食月」イスラム暦の9番目の月。イスラム教徒はこの月の間は日の出から日没まで断食する。

Keywords & Keypharases

本文に使われている次の語句の意味としてもっとも適切なものを a~j から選びなさい。

1. (l. 2) fast　　　　　a. 脱水症　　　　　1. (　)
2. (l. 5) opt to do　　 b. 糖尿病　　　　　2. (　)
3. (l. 7) in favor of　 c. 液体、水分　　　3. (　)
4. (l. 8) expedient　　 d. ブドウ糖　　　　4. (　)
5. (l. 13) diabetes　　 e. 賛否　　　　　　5. (　)
6. (l. 16) glucose　　　f. 断食する　　　　6. (　)

7.	(l. 20) dehydration	g.	〜することを選ぶ	7. (	)
8.	(l. 20) fluid	h.	厳密な	8. (	)
9.	(l. 32) rigorous	i.	適切な、ふさわしい	9. (	)
10.	(l. 32) pros and cons	j.	〜に賛成して	10. (	)

Exercises

1 本文中の空欄（ A ）,（ B ）,（ C ）に入る単語として最も適切なものをそれぞれ①〜③の中から選びなさい。

(A) ....
(B) ....
(C) ....

① and
② but
③ or

2 質問を読み、正しい答を (A) 〜 (D) の中から選びなさい。

Question 1

What is the overall view regarding fasting in this article?

(A) The dangers of fasting seem to outweigh its benefits.
(B) The religious custom of fasting is the best way to lose weight.
(C) The growing trend of fasting is backed by lots of scientific evidence.
(D) Fasting may have health benefits, but it is too early to be sure.

Question 2

According to the passage, what do some doctors question?

(A) The side-effects that result from fasting
(B) The types of regular meals people are eating
(C) The usefulness of fasting as a diet method
(D) The effectiveness of eating regular meals again

UNIT 3　Health

3 次の英文は本文の内容に関するものである。本文の内容に一致する場合は T を、一致しない場合は F を下線部に記入しなさい。

(A) According to the article, fasting is the best way to continue losing weight.

　　　　　　　　　　　　　　　　　　　　　　　　　　　　　　　　　　　．．．．．．．．．．．．．．．．．．．．

(B) The article explains one scientific reason why fasting leads to weight loss.

　　　　　　　　　　　　　　　　　　　　　　　　　　　　　　　　　　　．．．．．．．．．．．．．．．．．．．．

(C) According to the article, doctors are working to reduce the side-effects of fasting.　　　　　　　　　　　　　　　　　　　　　　　　　　　　　．．．．．．．．．．．．．．．．．．．．

4 次は本文の要約文である。空欄（ A),（ B),（ C),（ D ）に下記に与えられたアルファベットで始まる適切な 1-2 語を入れて要約文を完成させなさい。

More and more people in the United States and other countries are fasting on a regular basis for health reasons, rather than religious beliefs. People have been turning to fasting not only as a quick way to (A), but also for other apparent health benefits such as reducing (B). However, doctors have pointed out that there can be (C) health effects of fasting, too. In this way, it is not yet (D) whether fasting is a healthy option or not.

　　(A) l_____ w_____

　　(B) b_____ p_____

　　(C) n_____

　　(D) c_____

5 空所に入れる最も適切な語句を選択肢 (A) ～ (C) から選びなさい。

(1) 6対1の大差で、取締役会は合弁に賛成の決議を下した。

By a considerable, 6-to-1 margin, the board voted in (　　) of the joint venture.

(A) preference　　(B) favor　　(C) honor

(1) ....

(2) 子どもの肥満は糖尿病、心臓疾患、その他の健康障害を引き起こす。

Childhood obesity can cause (　　), heart disease, and other health problems.

(A) diagnosis　　(B) diabetes　　(C) depression

(2) ....

(3) あなたは安楽死についての賛否両論をいくつか読んだわけだが、あなたの考えは？

Now that you've read over several (　　) of mercy killing, what do you think?

(A) back and forth　　(B) ever and never　　(C) pros and cons

(3) ....

(4) 駐車制限や他の交通問題があるので、大会期間中は多くの人が自転車を使用することを選択している。

With parking restrictions and other traffic issues, many are (　　) to use bikes during the Convention.

(A) opting　　(B) addressing　　(C) applying

(4) ....

(5) 子どもの学年ごとの厳密な学習カリキュラムのサンプルは、ウェブサイトで見ることができます。

Examples of our (　　) academic curriculum at your child's grade level can be seen on the website.

(A) rigorous　　(B) preparatory　　(C) broad

(5) ....

Unit 4　History

カナダのゴールドラッシュ

The Klondike Gold Rush

ゴールドラッシュは実際はいろいろな国で起きている。1896年夏、カナダはアラスカ国境近く、クロンダイク地方で金鉱が発見されたといううわさが広がると、10万人以上がクロンダイクを目指した。だが、厳しい気候のせいで、到着できたのは3－4万人と言われている。500人足らずだったクロンダイクの人口は最盛期には3万人にまで膨れ上がった。しかし、運よく金を見つけて金持ちになったのは非常に少なく、多くは、金を見つけられずに病気になったり死亡した。

　One of the most storied periods in the history of North America was the Klondike Gold Rush, which took place in the Klondike* region of the Yukon* in northwest Canada. The gold rush lasted only three years (　　A　　) had a powerful impact upon the lives of the thousands of people who came to search for their fortunes.

　Gold was first discovered in the Klondike in the summer of 1896. This news spread like fire and over the next two years over 100,000 people trudged north in hopes of striking it rich on Klondike gold. Yet, the remoteness of the Klondike made it extremely difficult to reach. Prospectors had to come by western rivers (　　B　　) across steep mountain passes and the harsh conditions of winter limited the months of travel. In addition, because the area itself had few towns and no places to purchase survival items, the Canadian government required each new person to carry with them a one-year's supply of food. This meant each hopeful newcomer had to travel with almost one ton of personal goods. Still, they came!

The Yukon town of Dawson City* exploded in population from only 500 in 1896 to over 30,000 in 1898, an increase of six thousand percent. Other towns popped into existence out of nowhere. American author Jack London was one of the prospectors and later wrote about the madness of the gold rush in his novel, "The Call of the Wild*." The book also depicted the deadlier aspects of the frigid Klondike climate. Twenty years later, film star Charlie Chaplin also showed the desperation of the prospectors in his classic silent movie, "The Gold Rush*."

Both London's book and Chaplain's film tell the true story of the Klondike Gold Rush. Very few people ever found gold and got rich. Most struggled and a number lost everything they had. Many met disease in the crowded mining towns and sickness plus the cold winters cost many people their lives. While local residents profited initially by the flood of prospectors, the gold hunters also disrupted the environment and the Klondike was never the same after they left.

They left soon too. By 1899 the great Klondike Gold Rush was almost finished (C   ) the mining towns had mostly dried up and disappeared. The gold rush was an exciting moment that did not last, except within the hallowed pages of history books.

(395 words)

***Klondike** [klándàik] カナダ北西部を流れる川の名、およびその流域。　***Yukon** [júːkàn] カナダ北西部の連邦直轄地。　***Dawson City** クロンダイクのゴールドラッシュの時に建設された市。　*"**The Call of the Wild**" 『荒野の呼び声』1903年出版のジャック・ロンドンの代表作。　*"**The Gold Rush**" 『黄金狂時代』サイレント映画全盛時代の1925年に制作されたチャプリンの最高傑作ともいわれている映画。

Keywords & Keyphrases

本文に使われている次の語句の意味としてもっとも適切なものをa～jから選びなさい。

1.	(l. 7) trudge	a. 山道	1. (	)
2.	(l. 8) strike it rich	b. 採鉱者、金鉱を探す人	2. (	)
3.	(l. 9) prospector	c. 絶望	3. (	)
4.	(l. 10) pass	d. 神聖化された	4. (	)
5.	(l. 10) harsh	e. 厳しい、過酷な	5. (	)

UNIT 4　History

6. (l. 18) pop into existence　　f. 非常に寒い　　　　　　　　6. (　　)
7. (l. 21) frigid　　　　　　　　g. を崩壊させる　　　　　　　7. (　　)
8. (l. 22) desperation　　　　　h. とぼとぼ歩く、重い足取りで歩く　8. (　　)
9. (l. 28) disrupt　　　　　　　i. ひと山当てる　　　　　　　9. (　　)
10. (l. 31) hallowed　　　　　　j. 急に出現する　　　　　　　10. (　　)

Exercises

1 本文中の空欄（ A),(B),(C) に入る単語として最も適切なものを次の①〜③の中から選びなさい。

(A) ....
(B) ....
(C) ....

① and
② but
③ or

2 質問を読み、正しい答を (A)〜(D) の中から選びなさい。

Question 1

Which of the following statements best reflects the main idea of this passage?

(A) The Klondike Gold Rush was a short-lived but exciting event at the end of the 19th century.
(B) The Klondike Gold Rush inspired both books and movies.
(C) The Klondike Gold Rush was difficult due to the remote location of the Klondike.
(D) The Klondike Gold Rush changed the Klondike forever.

Question 2

What is one factor that made the remote Klondike region even harder to reach?

(A) Prospectors had to bring with them an enormous amount of supplies.
(B) The population in the Klondike grew steeply over a short time.
(C) The gold rush was limited to three short years.
(D) The Klondike suffered from fire in the summer of 1896.

3 次の英文は本文の内容に関するものである。本文の内容に一致する場合はTを、一致しない場合はFを下線部に記入しなさい。

(A) Local Klondike residents benefitted from the gold rush at first. ....

(B) A high percentage of people became wealthy thanks to discovering gold.

....

(C) There were basically two ways of reaching the remote Klondike region.

....

4 次は本文の要約文である。空欄（ A ），（ B ），（ C ），（ D ）に下記に与えられたアルファベットで始まる適切な語を入れて要約文を完成させなさい。

The Klondike Gold Rush only lasted three years, yet was a dramatic moment in the history of North America. During those (A) years over 100,000 people came to the remote Klondike in search of gold. The area was (B) to reach and prospectors had to carry their own supplies. The Klondike population shot upward, but (C) people found gold and the rush was over by 1899, three years after it began. While (D) in length, the Klondike Gold Rush inspired a famous book by Jack London and a renowned film by Charlie Chaplin.

(A) t ....

(B) h ....

(C) f ....

(D) s ....

UNIT 4 History

5 空所に入れる最も適切な語句を選択肢 (A) ～ (C) から選びなさい。

(1) その山道の最高部は2000メートル以上の標高だ。

The top of the (　) is more than two thousand meters high.

　(A) pass　　　　(B) road　　　　(C) swamp

(1) ....

(2) その騒乱により政府が過去4年間以上にわたってすすめてきた経済発展計画が混乱した。

The turmoil (　) the government's development plans in economy over the past four years.

　(A) disputed　　(B) dismissed　　(C) disrupted

(2) ....

(3) 7000人以上の兵士は雪と泥にまみれ、東へ200マイルも黄河河岸を目指して重い足取りで進んだ。

More than 7,000 soldiers (　) 200 miles east through snow and mud to the banks of the Yellow River.

　(A) trembled　　(B) transferred　　(C) trudged

(3) ....

(4) 我が国のほとんどは、長く寒い厳しい冬と比較的冷涼な短い夏といった気候である。

Most of our country has a (　) climate with long, cold winters and short, relatively cool summers.

　(A) harsh　　　(B) desert　　　(C) moist

(4) ....

(5) 昇進で希望がなくても、人生を楽しもうとすることはとても大切なことだ。

It's really important to try to enjoy your life in spite of the (　) in being promoted.

　(A) destiny　　(B) desperation　　(C) defect

(5) ....

Unit 5 Psychology

内気のすばらしさ

Are You Shy?

多くの人は Shy であることを一種の障害や弱点とみなしている。だが、shy であることには、じつは個人的にも社会的にも利点がある。例えば、Shy な人のほうが一生懸命に働いて、外向的な人がうまくできないことに成功することもある。また、社会は shy な人から多くの恩恵を受けている。shy な人は仕事にバランスをもたらし、集団に強い絆を育てる。社会には犯罪・暴力・差別など多くの問題があるが、もし、社会自身が shy な人たちのように控えめで思いやりのあるように変わっていけば、世界はもっとよくなるだろう。

About half of all people see themselves as "shy" in some way and many even view their timidity as a sort of handicap. They may look upon extroverts with envy and wish that they themselves were not so bashful. (A   ), this outlook may be mistaken, as being shy also has positive qualities that can benefit both individuals and society.

Of course, there are various levels of what might be defined as "shyness". These levels may range from a feeling of apprehension when meeting others to a severe inability to interact in any public situation. The condition may be genetic or it may be the result of abuse or teasing at some key period during childhood. Yet, except for extreme cases which might require counseling, shyness may not

UNIT 5   Pshycilogy

be the weakness that it is often perceived to be. Due to their typical unease with others, timid individuals are often motivated to work harder and can be driven to achieve where more outgoing people might fail. (　B　), being shy may serve as a vital aid in attaining success. The need to overcome shyness pushes people forward.

Shy individuals also bring positive traits to their schools and workplaces. Most such people are sensitive to the needs of others and have well-developed listening skills. They tend to weigh ideas carefully and make wise decisions. Society as a whole benefits from their ability to empathize with others. Shyer people bring balance to any endeavor and this balance allows groups to foster tighter relationships and move forward in a positive manner. Society would be less sensitive and caring if not for the perceptive nature of shy individuals.

(　C　), one adjective that might describe most shy people is the simple term, "nice." Society, on the other hand, often isn't nice at all. Crime, violence, discrimination — society has disturbing aspects that far too often end up dominating the nightly news. Our world might be a better place if, instead of shy people having to adjust to the crueler realities of society, society would instead adjust itself to the more modest and caring attitudes of the shy. Shy people can create a humbler, gentler and — yes — nicer environment for everyone.

Therefore, no one should think of their shy nature as a handicap. Instead, they should feel affirmed*! Shyness can be a positive trait and one well-needed* by humankind.

(389 words)

***feel affirmed**「肯定的に感じる」 ***well-needed**「十分必要とされた」

Keywords & Keypharases

本文に使われている次の語句の意味としてもっとも適切なものを a〜l から選びなさい。

1. (l. 2) timidity   a. 心配、不安   1. (　)
2. (l. 2) extrovert   b. 努力   2. (　)
3. (l. 3) bashful   c. 虐待；乱用   3. (　)
4. (l. 7) apprehension   d. 外向的な人   4. (　)
5. (l. 9) abuse   e. (人種) 差別、区別   5. (　)
6. (l. 9) tease   f. 臆病、小心   6. (　)
7. (l. 11) perceive   g. をからかう、をいじめる 7. (　)

8. (l. 16) trait	h. 特徴、特性	8. ( )
9. (l. 19) as whole	i. （〜であると）理解する、分かる	9. ( )
10. (l. 20) endeavor	j. 概して、全体として	10. ( )
11. (l. 22) perceptive	k. （知覚が）鋭い、鋭敏な	11. ( )
12. (l. 25) discrimination	l. 恥ずかしがり屋の、小心の	12. ( )

Exercises

1 本文中の空欄（ A),（ B),（ C ）に入る単語として最も適切なものを次の①〜③の中から選びなさい。

(A) ....
(B) ....
(C) ....

① Thus
② However
③ In fact

2 質問を読み、正しい答を (A) 〜 (D) の中から選びなさい。

Question 1

What is the key idea of this passage?

(A) In the worst cases, shy people may need counseling.
(B) Our world would be a better place if everyone was shy.
(C) Many people see shyness as negative, but it also has positive aspects.
(D) Shyness has different levels, but some are not so severe.

Question 2

According to this passage, why do many shy people tend to succeed?

(A) Because they are sensitive to the needs of others.
(B) Because they are motivated to overcome their shyness.
(C) Because their shyness was not as intense as they perceived it to be.
(D) Because they are often said to be very nice.

UNIT 5　Pshycilogy

3　次の英文は本文の内容に関するものである。本文の内容に一致する場合はTを、一致しない場合はFを下線部に記入しなさい。

(A) Groups can benefit from the listening skills and decision-making talents of shy people. ....

(B) Many people who suffer from being shy need counseling. ....

(C) This passage suggests the word "shy" could be replaced with "nice." ....

4　次は本文の要約文である。空欄(A), (B), (C), (D)に下記に与えられたアルファベットで始まる適切な語を入れて要約文を完成させなさい。

A large percentage of the population thinks of itself as "shy." But—except in advanced cases—this shyness (A) (B) be negative at all. Shy people work harder to adjust and often tend to be (C). They fit better into groups and make the world a gentler, more considerate place. Shyness should thus be considered a positive trait and not a (D).

(A) m....................

(B) n....................

(C) s....................

(D) h....................

5 空所に入れる最も適切な語句を選択肢 (A)〜(C) から選びなさい。

(1) 会社の業績は、ひとつの部門だけではなく全体として見ることが最も適切だ。

It is best to look at a company's performance (　　) instead of at only one department.

(A) as a whole　　(B) as it is　　(C) as they are

(1) ....

(2) その候補者は性差別に対し断固たる立場をとった。

That candidate took a firm stand against gender (　　).

(A) quality　　(B) differences　　(C) discrimination

(2) ....

(3) テレビの視聴者は性的虐待、不倫、そして DV に関するショッキングな告白にさらされている。

TV viewers are exposed to shocking confessions of sexual (　　), extra-marital affairs, and domestic violence.

(A) activity　　(B) abuse　　(C) issues

(3) ....

(4) ジョーは急いで階段を下りて父の部屋に飛び込み、その老人をからかっていたガキどもを追い払った。

Joe rushed downstairs into his father's room to scatter the gang of boys who were (　　) the old man.

(A) teasing　　(B) bullying　　(C) bashing

(4) ....

(5) 初日はいくばくかの不安と多くの同僚に会える興奮を感じながら席についた。

The first day I sat at the table with some (　　) and with excitement of seeing so many colleagues.

(A) apprehension　　(B) appreciation　　(C) anticipation

(5) ....

Unit 6　Animals

アメリカのペット・ビジネス

Pet Profits

　日本と同様、アメリカでもペット商品はビッグビジネスになっている。飼い主はペットを自分たちの子どもと考え、ペットを健康でハッピーにするために莫大なお金をつぎ込んでいる。例えば、特別な食べ物、しつけやお散歩代行といったサービス、さらには、ストレス軽減のセラピーまである。2008年以来、経済は停滞しているが、ペットのオーナー数は増大し続け、ペットを家族の一員とみなす考え方を背景に、ペットビジネスは伸び続けている。

　Products for pets like cats and dogs are now a big business in the United States. The variety of products and services now available to pet owners is increasing every year. More and more pet owners treat their pets as if they were their own children. As a result of this "pet parenting" attitude, people have become willing to spend a significant amount of money in an effort to make their pets healthy and happy.

　(　A　) in the past most people would buy cheap dog or cat food, today owners often pay much more to provide their beloved pet with a specialized diet. Many pet owners also pay for services to train or walk their dog — or even provide a dog with therapy to reduce stress.

Although the global economy has been in a recession ever since the 2008 financial crisis*, the pet industry has continued to prosper. Indeed, during the period from 2008 to 2013, the industry enjoyed 3.4% annual growth. In 2013, for example, around $55 billion* was spent on pet-related products and services, compared to around $43 billion in 2008. (　B　), not all pet stores have been doing well in recent years. Smaller stores, in particular, have had difficulty competing against the large retail chains. In the United States, two giant retail chains, PetSmart and PetCo, now account for about half of all revenue in the pet industry.

So what is the future outlook for the pet industry? Experts believe that the industry's growth will continue to be strong, at around 4% per year. One main factor that is expected to underlie that growth is the projected increase in the number of pet owners. According to some reports, the rate of pet ownership in the United States will increase by around 2.2% annually. By 2014, around 82.5 million American households owned pets, compared to 69 million in 2005 and just 51 million in 1998.

(　C　) the steady increase in pet owners is not the only factor behind the expected growth in the pet industry in the upcoming years. Another important factor is the increasing trend toward "pet parenting" already mentioned, which has increased demand for upscale products and services. Such specialty products and services represent the fastest growing segment within the pet industry. And this segment is expected to continue to expand as people increasingly view their pets as important family members.

(396 words)

the 2008 financial crisis** 2008年9月にアメリカの投資銀行リーマン・ブラザーズの破綻をきっかけに始まった世界的な金融危機のこと。$55 billion**「550億ドル」billion は10億、million（100万）の1,000倍。

Keywords & Keyphrases

本文に使われている次の語句の意味としてもっとも適切なものを a~i から選びなさい。

1. (l. 12) prosper　　　　a. 見通し、前途　　　　1. (　　)
2. (l. 17) retail　　　　　b. 部分、区分　　　　　2. (　　)
3. (l. 18) account for　　c. 所有者であること；所有権　3. (　　)
4. (l. 20) outlook　　　　d. の割合を占める　　　4. (　　)
5. (l. 22) underlie　　　e. 成長する、繁栄する　　5. (　　)

UNIT 6 Animals

6. (l. 23) ownership   f. の基にある、の根底にある   6. (   )
7. (l. 28) upcoming   g. もうすぐやって来る、来たる   7. (   )
8. (l. 30) upscale   h. 高級な；富裕層の   8. (   )
9. (l. 31) segment   i. 小売りの   9. (   )

Exercises

1 本文中の空欄（ A),（ B),（ C ）に入る単語として最も適切なものをそれぞれ①、②の中から選びなさい。

(A) ....
(B) ....
(C) ....

(A) ① Whereas   ② Because
(B) ① Therefore ② However
(C) ① And   ② But

2 質問を読み、正しい答を (A) 〜 (D) の中から選びなさい。

Question 1

What is the main purpose of this passage?

(A) To recommend good products for pets
(B) To predict the growth of the American pet industry
(C) To explain the history of the American pet industry
(D) To provide an overview of the American pet industry

Question 2

What is one trend in recent years in the pet industry?

(A) The number of pets increased by 51 million.
(B) The rate of pet ownership has increased by 3 to 4%.
(C) Smaller stores have struggled to compete with larger ones.
(D) People are spending around $40 billion a year on products and services.

3 次の英文は本文の内容に関するものである。本文の内容に一致する場合はTを、一致しない場合はFを下線部に記入しなさい。

(A) There is a trend toward children buying pets for the parents. ....

(B) The pet industry has done well despite the economic recession. ....

(C) The article points out that the future of the pet industry does not look bright.
....

4 次は本文の要約文である。空欄（ A ），（ B ），（ C ），（ D ）に下記に与えられたアルファベットで始まる適切な語を入れて要約文を完成させなさい。

The industry related to pet products and services is a big business in the United States. In recent years, the industry has been growing at around (A) to (B)% every year. The reasons for the (C) include the increasing number of pet owners and the trend toward treating pets like members of the (D). It seems likely that this growth will continue, at least in the near future.

(A) t..............................

(B) f..............................

(C) g..............................

(D) f..............................

UNIT 6 Animals

5 空所に入れる最も適切な語句を選択肢 (A)〜(C) から選びなさい。

(1) 人生に対して前向きな見通しをもっていれば、やることが楽しくなる。

Having a positive (　　) on life helps you enjoy the things you do.

(A) outcome　　　(B) outlook　　　(C) output

(1) ....

(2) ダニエルは100人の面前で近く行う発表のことで、とても緊張している。

Daniel is very nervous about his (　　) presentation in front of 100 people.

(A) upcoming　　　(B) ongoing　　　(C) following

(2) ....

(3) 人間は人生において固有の権利と義務を持っている、と彼は言った。それは、生活、自由、そして財産所有である。

He stated that people had particular rights and duties in life. These were life, liberty, and property (　　).

(A) assessment　　　(B) ownership　　　(C) rights

(3) ....

(4) 人間の骨格が体重の約50%を占めるかどうか知らない。

I don't know whether the human skeleton system (　　) for about 50 percent of the body weight.

(A) allows　　　(B) substitutes　　　(C) accounts

(4) ....

(5) 自由経済の根底にあるものは、選択したように行動ができるということである。

What really (　　) a free market is the ability to act as one chooses.

(A) underlies　　　(B) installs　　　(C) overlooks

(5) ....

Eating the Mediterranean Way

地中海料理は、肉を控えめにして、穀類・果物・ナッツ・野菜・魚を多く摂取し、また、オリーブオイル、ハーブの使用を特長としている。歴史的には19世紀半ばごろに医師 Ancel Keys が食事と健康の関係について調査研究を行い、ギリシャ人やイタリア人は、伝統的な食事に脂肪分が少なく、北ヨーロッパやアメリカ人より健康的であると結論付けている。だが、近年は動物性の脂肪摂取が多くなり、太りすぎの人が増大しているという。

Over the past two decades, many doctors and nutritionists have advocated the benefits of the "Mediterranean diet." This refers to the traditional cuisine in countries that border the Mediterranean Sea, such as Italy, Spain, and Greece.

What are the characteristics of the Mediterranean diet? Simply put, it is a diet on the consumption of a large quantity of grains, fresh fruit, nuts, vegetables, and seafood. Other aspects include replacing butter with healthy fats such as olive oil, using spices or herbs instead of salt, and limiting the amount of red meat consumed to just a few times a month.

One of the first doctors to recognize the benefits of this traditional way of eating in the Mediterranean was Ancel Keys*. In 1958, he began an ambitious research project called the Seven Countries Study that documented the eating habits of over 10,000 healthy middle-aged men living in Finland, Greece, Holland, Italy, Japan, the United States, and Yugoslavia. The study found that the heart-attack rates among these men corresponded to their diet and exercise habits.

His results also showed that men living in Greece and Italy tended to be healthier than those in Finland and the United States. Keys concluded that the diet consumed by Greeks and Italians included far (　A　) saturated fat than the food consumed in northern Europe or the United States.

Ironically, however, people living in countries like Greece, Italy, and Spain have been abandoning the Mediterranean diet in recent years. In particular, they are eating far (　B　) red meat and consuming more saturated fat. As a result of their changing dietary habits, obesity is on the rise in Mediterranean countries. This problem is particularly bad in Italy, where around 36% of Italian 12- to 16-year-olds are either overweight or obese.

Part of the reason why the Mediterranean diet was once so common in Italy and elsewhere was simply that people did not have enough money to eat red meat regularly. Now that these countries have become (　C　) affluent, people want to eat the kind of food that was once only consumed by the rich. Another major factor is the rise of the fast-food industry throughout Europe. But increasingly southern Europeans are recognizing the value of their traditional diet.

Ancel Keys himself ate according to the Mediterranean diet — and he lived to the age of 101. When asked if he attributed his longevity to this diet, he responded: "Very likely, but no proof." (405 words)

*Ancel Keys　アンセル・キーズ。アメリカの生理学者。

Keywords & Keypharases

本文に使われている次の語句の意味としてもっとも適切なものを a~j から選びなさい。

1. (l. 1) nutritionist　　a. 長寿、長生き　　　　　　1. (　)
2. (l. 1) advocate　　　 b. 栄養学者、栄養士　　　　2. (　)
3. (l. 11) document　　 c. に対応する、に相応する　3. (　)
4. (l. 14) correspond to　d. …の原因を〜のせいにする　4. (　)
5. (l. 18) saturated　　　e. を唱える、を主張する　　5. (　)

6. (l. 23) dietary	f. を立証する、を記録する	6. ( )
7. (l. 25) obese	g. 裕福な、豊かな	7. ( )
8. (l. 28) affluent	h. 飽和した、いっぱいの	8. ( )
9. (l. 34) attribute ... to	i. 肥満した、太りすぎの	9. ( )
10. (l. 34) longevity	j. 食事の、食事に関する	10. ( )

Exercises

1 本文中の空欄 (A), (B), (C) には "more" または "less" が入る。more が入るときは ①を、less が入るときは②を下の空欄に書き入れなさい。

(A) ....
(B) ....
(C) ....

① more
② less

2 質問を読み、正しい答を (A) 〜 (D) の中から選びなさい。

Question 1

What is the main purpose of this article?

  (A) To recommend a good way to lose weight
  (B) To introduce one healthy dietary tradition
  (C) To examine changes in diets in the Mediterranean
  (D) To present the life of the famous doctor Ancel Keys

Question 2

What did Ancel Keys conclude from his Seven Countries Study?

  (A) Men in northern Europe were not exercising enough.
  (B) Southern Europeans tended to eat less saturated fat.
  (C) People in Greece and Italy ate less food than in other countries.
  (D) Finland and the United States switched to the Mediterranean diet.

UNIT 7 Food

3 次の英文は本文の内容に関するものである。本文の内容に一致する場合はTを、一致しない場合はFを下線部に記入しなさい。

(A) Ancel Keys has studied the Mediterranean Diet over the past two decades.

....

(B) The Mediterranean diet uses olive oil instead of butter.　....................

(C) Italians are becoming overweight despite following the Mediterranean diet.

....

4 次は本文の要約文である。空欄(A), (B)には適切な1-2語を入れ、(C)には選択肢①、②から適切な語（句）を書き入れなさい。

Many doctors and nutritionists believe that the "Mediterranean diet" is a healthy way of eating. This type of cuisine involves a lot of grains, fruit, nuts, vegetables, and seafood—and limiting (A) and (B). Ancel Keys was one of the first doctors to recognize the benefits of this diet based on his study of people living in seven different countries. Unfortunately, in many Mediterranean countries, people are (C) eating in the traditional way.

(A) ....　..................................

(B) ....

(C) ....　[① still　② no longer]

5 空所に入れる最も適切な語句を選択肢 (A) ～ (C) から選びなさい。

(1) なぜ私が核兵器の廃絶を主張するためにここにいるのか、説明させてください。

Let me tell you why I am here to (　　) the abolition of nuclear weapons.

　(A) advocate　　　(B) treat　　　　　(C) engage

(1) ....

(2) あなたの給料が、労働時間数に見合うだけ支払われていることを確認しなさい。

Check that your pay (　　) to the number of hours you worked.

　(A) corresponds　　(B) matches　　　(C) stands

(2) ....

(3) こぎれいな身なりで礼儀正しく、彼は裕福なビジネスマンのように見えた。

Beautifully dressed and well-mannered, he looked like (　　) businessman.

　(A) a competent　　(B) a potential　　(C) an affluent

(3) ....

(4) 売上げの不振は、しばしばマーケティング活動の失敗のせいにされうる。

Low sales can often be (　　) to poor marketing

　(A) expressed　　(B) attributed　　(C) called

(4) ....

(5) 腎臓病が進行すると、食事で必要なものもおそらく変化します。

As your kidney disease progresses, your (　　) needs will likely change as well.

　(A) nutritional　　(B) dietary　　(C) material

(5) ....

Unit 8　Art

芸術のハブ都市ニューヨーク

New York as Artistic Hub

19世紀から20世紀初めごろまで、芸術の中心はパリであった。ところが1929年に始まった世界大恐慌は世界中に広がり、世界は長い間、不況に苦しむ時代を迎える。こうした状況下、世界大戦が起こり、アメリカ経済は New York を中心に活況を呈することになる。これに対し、ヨーロッパは不況から抜け出せず、サルバドール・ダリをはじめ、多くの芸術家がヨーロッパから New York に移住してくる。こうして、アートの中心はパリから New York へ移っていくのである。

　New York today is a center of the financial world, but the city is also an important hub of the art world. But it has not always been an artistic center. Throughout the 19th century and early 20th century, Paris was the undisputed capital of artistic and intellectual life in the world. By the time that World War II ended in 1945, however, New York had replaced the French capital as the center　5 of the world's artistic production and consumption.

　One obvious reason that New York emerged as a dynamic center for the arts in the 1940s was related to economic factors. During the previous decade, the city's economy had been stagnant (　A　) the Great Depression*, but the increased demand for production during the war helped restore prosperity. Paris　10 and other European cities faced tough economic times after the war, whereas the economy was booming in postwar New York. This strong economy attracted many artists and art dealers to the city from Paris.

 Another key factor was that numerous artists and intellectuals migrated from Europe to New York during the late 1930s and early 1940s to escape from the war. These talented immigrants helped to quickly raise the level of cultural life in New York. Some famous modernist and avant-garde* artists also moved to New York in pursuit of artistic freedom. Some of the renowned European artists who spent time in New York during the war period included Arshile Gorky, Marcel Duchamp, Max Ernst, and Salvador Dalí*.

 New York became famous for its abstract paintings in particular. These were works of art that focused on shapes and colors, rather than the representation of real things. The artists centered in New York who embraced this approach to painting came to be known as the "abstract expressionists*." The most famous American painter in this movement was Jackson Pollock*. He was famous for his innovative style of "action painting*," which involved creating designs by dripping painting on the canvas, (　B　) painting directly on it with a brush.

 (　C　) the success of these abstract painters—and the "Pop Art*" painters who came later—the reputation of New York as the capital of art became firmly established, and the city remains one of the main destinations for aspiring artists.

(379 words)

*the Great Expression「大恐慌」1929年アメリカニューヨーク市場の暴落から始まった世界的大恐慌。 *avant-garde [àvɑ̀ːn(t)gɑ́ːd]「前衛派（の）」新しい芸術運動の実践者。フランス語の「アヴァンギャルド（前衛）」から。 *Arshile Gorky [ɑ́ːrʃil góːrki] アーシル・ゴーリキー (1904–48)。アルメニア出身の画家。 *Marcel Duchamp [mɑːrsél d(j)uʃɑ̃ː] マーセル・デュシャン (1887–1968)。フランスの画家。 *Max Ernst [mǽks ɑ́ːrst] マックス・エルンスト (1891–1976)。ドイツ出身の画家。後年フランスに帰化。 *Salvador Dali [sǽlvədɔː dɑ́ːli] サルバヴァドール・ダリ (1904–89)。スペイン生まれのシュールレアリスムの画家。 *abstract expressionists「抽象表現主義派」作家の主観的感情表現を追求しようとする画家たちの呼称。 *Jackson Pollock ジャクソン・ポロック (1912–56)。絵の具を上からたらす drip painting の技法を展開した。 *action painting「アクション・ペインティング」描く行為そのものを重要視する抽象画の一様式。 *Pop Art「ポップ・アート」1950年代の後半からアメリカを中心におこった、広告や漫画などから派生した前衛的美術運動。

Keywords & Keyphrases

本文に使われている次の語句の意味としてもっとも適切なものを a~k から選びなさい。

1. (l. 2) hub	a. 表現主義者、表現派	1. (　　)
2. (l. 3) undisputed	b. 表現すること、描写	2. (　　)
3. (l. 9) stagnant	c. 中心地、拠点	3. (　　)

UNIT 8　Art

4.　(l. 12)　boom
5.　(l. 18)　in pursuit of
6.　(l. 18)　renowned
7.　(l. 22)　representation
8.　(l. 23)　embrace
9.　(l. 24)　expressionist
10.　(l. 27)　drip
11.　(l. 30)　aspiring

d.　を含める；を採用する
e.　にわかに景気づく；繁栄する
f.　滴る、ポタポタ落ちる
g.　野心のある、意欲的な
h.　議論の余地のない、明白な
i.　名高い、有名な
j.　不景気な、停滞した
k.　〜を求めて

4.　(　　)
5.　(　　)
6.　(　　)
7.　(　　)
8.　(　　)
9.　(　　)
10.　(　　)
11.　(　　)

Exercises

1 本文中の空欄（ A),(B),(C) に入る単語として最も適切なものをそれぞれ①、②の中から選びなさい。

(A) ....
(B) ....
(C) ....

(A)　① in spite of　② because of
(B)　① as well as　② rather than
(C)　① Thanks to　② But for

2 質問を読み、正しい答を (A) 〜 (D) の中から選びなさい。

Question 1

What is the main topic of this passage?

(A) The expansion of New York during World War II
(B) The famous modernist artists who moved to New York
(C) The rivalry between Paris and New York as artistic hubs
(D) The story of how New York became a center for art

Question 2

What is one thing that happened during World War II?

(A) Jackson Pollock invented action painting.
(B) New York's avant-garde artists became famous.
(C) Many artists and intellectuals moved to New York.
(D) New York's economy started booming thanks to the art market.

3 次の英文は本文の内容に関するものである。本文の内容に一致する場合はTを、一致しない場合はFを下線部に記入しなさい。

(A) Many art dealers left Paris for New York after World War II. ....

(B) A desire for artistic freedom attracted some famous artists to New York.
....

(C) Most of the famous abstract expressionists were from Paris. ....

4 次は本文の要約文である。空欄（ A ）〜（ E ）に入れるべき適切な語（句）を①〜⑤から選び、必要に応じて適切な活用形にして要約文を完成させなさい。なお、2度使う選択肢がある。

Paris was once the art capital of the world, but that changed in the 1940s when many artists and art dealers (A) New York. Many artists (B) New York to (C) the war; others were attracted by the city's booming economy. New York (D) a center for abstract art by such artists as Jackson Pollock. Even today, New York (E) an important artistic center.

(A) ....

(B) ....

(C) ....

(D) ....

(E) ....

| ① become | ② change to | ③ escape |
| ④ move to | ⑤ remain | |

UNIT 8　Art

5　空所に入れる最も適切な語句を選択肢 (A) ～ (C) から選びなさい。

(1) ABC コーポレーションは丸 1 年間の売り上げの不振と利益の減少を警告した。

ABC Corporation has warned of (　　) sales and reduced profits for its full year.

　　(A) regional　　　　(B) initial　　　　(C) stagnant

(1) ....

(2) 1928 年のアメリカ株式市場はにわか景気に沸き、信用買いは当たり前となった。

In 1928 the stock market in the U.S. was (　　) and buying on margin became commonplace.

　　(A) booming　　　　(B) targeting　　　　(C) consuming

(2) ....

(3) 多くの移民と彼らの家族は繁栄を求めてブラジルにやって来た。

Many immigrants and their families come to Brazil (　　) prosperity.

　　(A) in return for　　(B) in pursuit of　　(C) with a chance for

(3) ....

(4) 世界的に有名なシンガー、ソングライター、レコードプロデューサー、ダンサーであるマイケル・ジャクソンは、2009 年、50 歳で亡くなっている。

Michael Jackson, internationally (　　) singer, songwriter, record producer and dancer, dies at 50 in 2009.

　　(A) featured　　　　(B) aspiring　　　　(C) renowned

(4) ....

(5) 多くの企業は顧客に情報を伝える手段としてインターネットを採用している。

Many companies have (　　) the Internet as a means of distributing information to customers.

　　(A) provided　　　　(B) embraced　　　　(C) inspired

(5) ....

Unit 9　Biography

世紀の大悪党ジョン・デリンジャー

John Dillinger—Public Enemy No. 1

　アメリカには多くのギャングヒーローがいるが、ジョン・デリンジャーもその一人である。大恐慌の1930年代を背景に、デリンジャーは銀行強盗を12回、警察署からの武器等強奪を2回行い、何度か捉えられてもその都度なぜか脱獄した。大不況に苦しむ国民は、当時、政府や銀行を信用しておらず、政府や銀行に立ち向かったデリンジャーはヒーローとして喝采を浴びた。その人気は定着し、デリンジャーを扱った映画は10本を超えている。

　John Dillinger was a criminal so dangerous that the American government branded him Public Enemy No. 1*, the first person ever to earn that dubious honor. Yet, at the same time, he was also a national hero, admired by thousands of people across the nation. Such was the unusual impact of the most notorious bank robber in American history.

　Starting in 1933*, Dillinger and his gang robbed twelve banks. They also attacked and plundered two police stations, stealing guns, ammunition and even bulletproof vests. Although once apprehended, Dillinger somehow escaped jail while under heavy guard. This incredible string of success—all within a single year—made people think he was invincible. His reign of success came during the worst days of the Great Depression. Many people were struggling to eke out a living and felt powerless in their lives. Dillinger was breaking the law, but he was also taking action against forces that common people now saw as untrustworthy — the government and banks — and thus he became a hero.

Dillinger's image was also helped by the developments in mass media. (A), many American homes now had radios and news spread quickly. If Dillinger robbed a bank one day, it was broadcast across the land the next*. (B), police methods were not so well-developed. There was not yet a national database of fingerprints and security cameras had not even been invented. It was thus easy for criminals to escape and hide. (C), many people did not want Dillinger to be caught. While in jail, he was interviewed by reporters and he came across as personable and funny. So people cheered him.

Yet, he was clearly a threat to public safety. In June of 1934 Dillinger was declared Public Enemy No. 1. One month later, federal agents* cornered Dillinger after he left a movie theater in Chicago. He tried to run and was shot dead*. Still, many people could not believe he had been killed. A legend spread that the police had gunned down the wrong man and Dillinger was still free. However, no one ever saw him again.

Criminal or celebrity? John Dillinger was both. Proof of this can be seen by his reception by the film industry. Dillinger and his gang have served as inspiration for over ten Hollywood movies. America has never had a criminal as infamous as John Dillinger.

(401 words)

*Public Enemy No.1 「大悪党」 *starting in 1933 「1933 年に始まって」 *the next =the next day *federal agents 「連邦捜査局 (FBI) の捜査員たち」 *was shot dead 「銃で撃たれて死んだ」

Keywords & Keyphrases

本文に使われている次の語句の意味としてもっとも適切なものを a~l から選びなさい。

1. (l. 2) brand   a. 時代、治世   1. (   )
2. (l. 2) dubious   b. 銃弾、弾薬   2. (   )
3. (l. 7) plunder   c. を追い詰める、を追い込む   3. (   )
4. (l. 7) ammunition   d. をやりくりする、に苦労する 4. (   )
5. (l. 8) bulletproof   e. (〜悪いものと) 決めつける 5. (   )
6. (l. 8) apprehend   f. (〜から) 物を略奪する   6. (   )
7. (l. 10) invincible   g. を捕まえる、を逮捕する   7. (   )

John Dillinger—Public Enemy No. 1

8. (l. 10) reign	h. ～という印象を与える	8. ( )
9. (l. 11) eke out	i. 怪しげな；いかがわしい	9. ( )
10. (l. 22) come across as	j. 品のある	10. ( )
11. (l. 22) personable	k. 防弾の	11. ( )
12. (l. 24) corner	l. 無敵の；征服できない	12. ( )

Exercises

1 本文中の空欄（ A),(B),(C ）に入る単語として最も適切なものをそれぞれ①〜③の中から選びなさい。

(A) ....
(B) ....
(C) ....

① At the same time
② In fact
③ Unlike earlier days

2 質問を読み、正しい答を (A) 〜 (D) の中から選びなさい。

Question 1

Which sentence best describes this passage?

(A) John Dillinger was the most notorious criminal in American history.
(B) John Dillinger became nationally renowned due to all his criminal success.
(C) John Dillinger was eventually caught and shot by lawmen.
(D) John Dillinger drew acclaim from the public even though he was a dangerous bank robber.

Question 2

What was one factor that helped create John Dillinger's positive public image?

(A) He and his gang helped struggling and powerless people.
(B) A legend grew that he wasn't killed but escaped yet again.
(C) He became the first Public Enemy No. 1 in history.
(D) In interviews he seemed likeable and humorous.

UNIT 9　Biography

3 次の英文は本文の内容に関するものである。本文の内容に一致する場合はTを、一致しない場合はFを下線部に記入しなさい。

(A) John Dillinger was an active bank robber for about one year.　　...................

(B) The public followed Dillinger's criminal career in the news, as if he were a celebrity.　　...................

(C) John Dillinger was shot by federal agents in Chicago while he was trying to surrender.　　...................

4 次は本文の要約文である。空欄（　A　）～（　F　）に入れるべき適切なものを①～⑥から選んで要約文を完成させなさい。

John Dillinger (　A　) America's most famous criminal due to a combination of successful robberies and intense media coverage, which showed him in a positive light. His activities were thus (　B　) by people suffering economic hardship during the Great Depression. These people (　C　) Dillinger as fighting against the system that (　D　) the Depression. The police had trouble locating Dillinger, but finally (　E　) him on the streets of Chicago. Even after he died, many people (　F　) Dillinger had escaped and was still free.

(A) ....

(B) ....

(C) ....

(D) ....

(E) ....

(F) ....

① became
② believed
③ caused
④ cheered
⑤ killed
⑥ saw

John Dillinger—Public Enemy No. 1

5 空所に入れる最も適切な語句を選択肢 (A) ～ (C) から選びなさい。

(1) イタリアの怪しい各種報道によれば、ミスター G はマンチェスター・ユナイテッドの次期マネージャーになるという。

Mr. G is said to become the next manager of Manchester United, according to (　　) reports in Italy.

  (A) deliberate   (B) valid   (C) dubious

                         (1) ....

(2) シリア、パルミラの国立美術館は、ISIS の兵士によって完全に略奪されていた。

The national museum in Syria's Palmyra has been completely (　　) by the ISIS militants.

  (A) ascended   (B) comprised   (C) plundered

                         (2) ....

(3) 1930 年代のアメリカ合衆国では、約 100 万人が捕えられてメキシコに送られた。

In the United States during the 1930s, about a million people were (　　) and sent to Mexico.

  (A) recruited   (B) apprehended   (C) preserved

                         (3) ....

(4) ムーア人の治世において町の周囲につくられた豪華な赤いレンガの壁は、いまだ現存している。

The gorgeous red brick wall built around the city during the Moors' (　　) still exists.

  (A) reign   (B) token   (C) cabinet

                         (4) ....

(5) 無敵の宇宙戦艦ヤマトとその乗組員は、政府のために次々と勝利をもたらした。

(　　) spaceship Yamato and its crew have delivered a string of victories for their government.

  (A) Notable   (B) Invincible   (C) Decisive

                         (5) ....

Unit 10 Tourism

ハワイの隠れた名所

The Attraction of Kealakekua Bay

Kealakekua Bay はハワイ島の西側に位置する小さな湾だが、車でのアクセスはできず、多くの人は海路でこの湾を訪れる。湾での魅力はシュノーケリング。熱帯魚が 700 種以上も生息し、愛好家のパラダイスである。歴史的には 18 世紀後半にイギリス人冒険家、ジェームズ・クックがハワイ島を発見し、ヨーロッパに紹介したが、その後、先住民との戦いで命を落とすことになる。作家マーク・トゥエインは約 100 年後にここを訪れ、非業の死をとげたクックを偲んだという。

　Kealakekua Bay* on the western coast of the island of Hawaii offers tourists a unique combination of history and sea sport activity. The bay — pronounced — Kay-ah-lah-kay-koo-ah — is located only 12 miles south of the popular Hawaiian city of Kona*, yet (　A　) be reached by car. The only access is by hiking overland or by venturing out on the waves by either kayak or tour boat. Most visitors choose these (　B　) means because the 12-mile ocean trip offers a stunning view of the Hawaiian coast and also affords chances to spot dolphins or occasionally even whales frolicking in the open sea. Once in the mild water of the tiny bay, visitors can then enjoy some of the finest snorkeling in the world.

　The waters* of the bay — green and tranquil on the surface — present an entirely different view underneath. The sea below teams with* darting tropical fish, in hues of yellow, blue, red and more. In fact, over 700 different varieties of tropical fish swim in Hawaiian waters with many of these to be found only in Hawaii. The bay is thus a snorkeler's paradise and (C) visitor leaves unimpressed by the vibrant colors of the fish as they flash in and around the coral. An afternoon or morning at Kealakekua Bay might well become the highlight of any stop* in Hawaii.

Kealakekua Bay is also a key historical spot, as it was here in 1779 that renowned British explorer James Cook was killed in a clash with native Hawaiians. Beginning in 1766, Cook made three voyages to the Pacific and these journeys helped promote western knowledge of the globe. Cook thus became a hero to adventure-minded youth throughout the English-speaking world. In fact, about 100 years later, in 1866, American author Mark Twain traveled to Kealakekua Bay just to visit the spot of Cook's untimely death. In his writings, Twain states that he observed the site from a flat stone at the bay's edge and, while no one can be certain, even now there lies a wide flat rock where Mark Twain possibly stood as he imagined the bitter fate of his hero, James Cook.

Today Kealakekua Bay sports a 27-foot high white monument in memory of Captain Cook. The modern tourist, however, may be more interested in what is below the waves. Yet, history and nature go together well at Kealakekua Bay. It's a place that all visitors to Hawaii should add to their itinerary.   (411 words)

*Kealakekua Bay [keiàːləkəkúː-] ケアラケクア湾。　*Kona [kóunə] コナ。海水浴場で有名。
*the waters　特定の海・川・湖の水。後出の Hawaiian waters は「ハワイの水域」の意味。
*team with ...「…とチームを組ませる」　*stop「(一時的な)滞在」

Keywords & Keyphrases

本文に使われている次の語句の意味としてもっとも適切なものを a~l から選びなさい。

1.	(l. 5) overland	a. 色、色合い	1. ( )
2.	(l. 5) venture out	b. 旅程表	2. ( )
3.	(l. 7) stunning	c. はしゃぐ、浮かれ騒ぐ	3. ( )
4.	(l. 8) occasionally	d. サッと動く、素早く動く	4. ( )
5.	(l. 8) frolic	e. を見せる、を展示する	5. ( )
6.	(l. 11) dart	f. 危険を冒して行く	6. ( )
7.	(l. 12) hue	g. 早すぎる；時期尚早な	7. ( )

UNIT 10 Tourism

8. (l. 15) vibrant   h. 色鮮やかな；活気のある   8. (   )
9. (l. 19) renowned   i. 名高い、有名な   9. (   )
10. (l. 24) untimely   j. すばらしい、魅力的な   10. (   )
11. (l. 28) sport   k. 陸路で   11. (   )
12. (l. 31) itinerary   l. 時には、たまに   12. (   )

Exercises

1 本文中の空欄 (A), (B), (C) に入る単語として最も適切なものをそれぞれ①、②の中から選びなさい。

(A) ....
(B) ....
(C) ....

(A) ① can   ② cannot
(B) ① former   ② latter
(C) ① some   ② no

2 質問を読み、正しい答を (A) 〜 (D) の中から選びなさい。

Question 1

What two features make Kealakekua Bay a tourist attraction?

(A) This was where James Cook died and Mark Twain once visited.
(B) The bay is great for snorkeling and there is a rock where Mark Twain perhaps stood.
(C) James Cook died here and the bay has a monument dedicated to snorkeling.
(D) The bay is popular with snorkelers and it is also the spot where James Cook died.

Question 2

According to this passage, what is the most popular way to visit Kealakekua Bay?

(A) By car
(B) By sea
(C) By hiking
(D) By snorkeling

3 次の英文は本文の内容に関するものである。本文の内容に一致する場合はTを、一致しない場合はFを下線部に記入しなさい。

(A) The rock where Mark Twain stood has been clearly identified. ....

(B) Kealakekua Bay is known for dolphins and occasionally whales. ....

(C) Most modern visitors are more interested in Captain Cook than snorkeling.
....

4 次は本文の要約文である。空欄（ A),(B),(C),(D ）に入れるべき適切なものを①〜④から選んで要約文を完成させなさい。

Kealakekua Bay is a small bay on the western coast of the island of Hawaii. It offers two tourist treats* in that it is both (A) and it is also the place where famed explorer James Cook met his death over 230 years ago. Visitors to Kealakekua Bay can snorkel in (B) or, like writer Mark Twain once did, they can look with awe on (C). Cook is now honored with (D) that stands at Kealakekua Bay.

* **treat** 楽しみ、喜び

(A) ....
(B) ....
(C) ....
(D) ....

> ① the calm waters
> ② a major snorkeling site
> ③ a tall monument
> ④ a rare historical site

UNIT 10　Tourism

5　空所に入れる最も適切な語句を選択肢 (A) 〜 (C) から選びなさい。

(1) スピーチの間、私はメモをたまにチラッと見ただけだった。

I only glanced at my notes (　　) during my speech.

　　(A) eventually　　　(B) rarely　　　(C) occasionally

(1) ....

(2) 旅程表で待ち合わせ時間を確認し、遅れることのないようにしてください。

Please check the meeting times on your travel (　　) and make sure you are not late.

　　(A) stationery　　　(B) transition　　　(C) itinerary

(2) ....

(3) 彼らは壊れやすい船で極寒の海に危険を冒して乗り出すべきではなかった。

They should not have (　　) out in fragile boats in frigid waters.

　　(A) ventured　　　(B) captured　　　(C) aspired

(3) ....

(4) 私の町は 1990 年代に活気のある小さなシーサイドリゾートに再生した。

My town regenerated into a (　　) small seaside resort in the 1990s.

　　(A) valid　　　(B) vibrant　　　(C) vital

(4) ....

(5) おいしい朝食をとりながら、すばらしい山の眺めをご堪能ください。

Take in the (　　) mountain views while you enjoy a gourmet breakfast.

　　(A) remaining　　　(B) stunning　　　(C) renowned

(5) ....

Unit 11 Social Problem

卑劣なネットいじめ

Cyber-Bullying

いじめは以前から学校や職場で非難されてきたが、インターネットの発達により、いわゆる「ネットいじめ」が増大している。ネットユーザーは名前を隠したり、偽名を使うことができるので、加害者は特定されづらく、攻撃性を増大させている。最近はスマートフォンは生活必需品となっているので、ネットの世界自体から逃れることもできない。決定的な解決策は難しいが、「誰も他人を傷つける権利はない」という教育を徹底させるのが最善のソリューションだろう。

　Bullying — the deliberate harm or harassment of targeted individuals or groups — has long been condemned in schools and work places around the world. Yet our new information society and the increase of social networking has given birth to a new form of bullying — cyber-bullying. While never physical, in many ways cyber-bullying can be just as painful as regular bullying. More than this, it can be much harder to stop.

　A regular bully can rarely hide. His or her actions or words are often in the open. Yet, a cyber-bully operates under the anonymity of the Internet. Such bullies can use temporary email accounts, false names, and instant messaging services* to completely hide their identity. Victims may (　　A　　) know the

UNIT 11 Social Problem

person who is harassing them. This anonymity can encourage the cyber-bully to write or post increasingly harmful messages. The bullying can thus be intense, applying vile* and venomous* language no one would (B   ) use in public.

Because social media and chat rooms are largely unsupervised, cyber-bullies often feel free to do as they please. There is no one to police their words and they may see themselves as being impossible to trace. Even teens under strict parental guidance may feel (C   ) restraint, as they may be more computer-savvy* than their parents and thus easily avoid the scrutiny of their mother's and father's eyes. While they might never bully someone in public, they might find it simple to do so online. They also never see the pain they cause. Cyber-bullying can become like an action game, one of attacking and then hiding, with the bully thinking only of his or her own fun.

With a real bully, the victim can usually find some escape. For example, if bullied at school, the victim can opt not to attend classes. Yet these days more and more people are dependent on their cellular phones. They may need their phones for business or class and cannot discard them so readily. Changing email addresses or staying away from certain chat rooms are possible solutions, but this can be troublesome for the bullied person. More than this, it may not stop the bullying. Cyber-bullies are never sure who is viewing their posts and may continue to spread damaging information even if their target is not reading. Other people will see it and thus the victim is still slandered* and hurt.

Cyber-bullying remains difficult to stop. Perhaps the best weapon against it is education. People must be taught that no one has the right to hurt others in any environment. Never become a cyber-bully! (428 words)

෴෴෴෴෴෴෴෴෴෴
***instant messaging services** インターネットに接続している人にリアルタイムでメッセージを送るサービス。 ***vile** 「汚い、下劣な」 ***venomous** 「悪意[敵意]に満ちた」 ***computer-savvy** 「コンピューターに精通した」 ***slander** 「を中傷する」

Keywords & Keypharases

本文に使われている次の語句の意味としてもっとも適切なものを a~l から選びなさい。

1.	(l. 1) bullying	a. 匿名（性）	1. (	)
2.	(l. 1) deliberate	b. 制限；自制	2. (	)
3.	(l. 2) condemn	c. いじめをする人、いじめっ子	3. (	)
4.	(l. 7) bully	d. いじめ、中傷	4. (	)

5. (l. 8) anonymity   e. 監視；綿密な調査   5. (   )
6. (l. 11) harass   f. を監視する、を取り締まる   6. (   )
7. (l. 12) intense   g. に嫌がらせをする、を悩ます 7. (   )
8. (l. 14) unsupervised   h. 非難する；有罪の判決を出す 8. (   )
9. (l. 15) police   i. を捨てる、を廃棄する   9. (   )
10. (l. 17) restraint   j. 激しい、極端な   10. (   )
11. (l. 18) scrutiny   k. 監視されていない   11. (   )
12. (l. 26) discard   l. 故意の   12. (   )

Exercises

1 本文中の空欄（ A),(B),(C ）に入る単語として最も適切な語をそれぞれ①〜③の中から選びなさい。

(A) ....
(B) ....
(C) ....

(A) ① ever   ② never
(B) ① ever   ② never
(C) ① little   ② much

2 質問を読み、正しい答を (A) 〜 (D) の中から選びなさい。

Question 1

What does this passage attempt to explain?

(A) The history and development of cyber-bullying
(B) How cyber-bullying can be worse than regular bullying
(C) The difficulty of catching a cyber-bully
(D) How to condemn cyber-bullying.

Question 2

Why is changing one's email address not a full solution in stopping a cyber-bully?

(A) Changing one's email address is troublesome.
(B) Cyber-bullies can hide under false names.
(C) Cyber-bullies will continue anyway.
(D) Cyber-bullies can usually avoid the scrutiny of others.

UNIT 11 Social Problem

3 次の英文は本文の内容に関するものである。本文の内容に一致する場合はTを、一致しない場合はFを下線部に記入しなさい。

(A) Victims typically know who is troubling them. ....

(B) Cyber-bullies often feel confident that they cannot be caught. ....

(C) Victims are often too dependent on their cellular phones to give them up.

....

4 次は本文の要約文である。空欄(A), (B), (C), (D)に入れるべき適切な語句を①〜④から選んで要約文を完成させなさい。

Cyber-bullying is a form of bullying that involves (A) of people or peoples via the Internet. Cyber-bullying may be worse than standard bullying due to the anonymity of (B) and (C) that the Internet is often free from supervision*. In addition, people these days are highly dependent on their cellular phones, making it difficult to avoid a cyber-bully's attacks. In the end, cyber-bullies may not care who reads what they post so (D) cannot truly escape. The best way to stop cyber-bullying seems to be education.

〰〰〰〰〰〰〰〰〰〰
* **supervision** 監視；管理

(A) ....
(B) ....
(C) ....
(D) ....

| ① the victim |
| ② the bully |
| ③ the fact |
| ④ the harassment |

5 空所に入れる最も適切な語句を選択肢 (A) ～ (C) から選びなさい。

(1) 円を回復させることは意図的な処置だった。

It was a (　) measure to cause the yen to recover.

(A) deliberate　　　(B) subordinate　　　(C) legitimate

(1) ....

(2) そのストライキは、2日間にわたる激しい交渉の末に回避された。

The strike was averted after two days of (　) negotiations.

(A) mortal　　　(B) plain　　　(C) intense

(2) ....

(3) 予算の制限により公立図書館の営業時間は変更せざるを得ない。

The hours of the Public Library have to be altered due to budget (　).

(A) restraints　　　(B) transactions　　　(C) abortion

(3) ....

(4) アパレル会社のゼップは、議論の的になっている広告のせいで注視されている。

The clothing company Zep is under (　) for a controversial ad.

(A) scheme　　　(B) applause　　　(C) scrutiny

(4) ....

(5) その新しいタイプのエネルギーは、昔は捨てられていたゴミから作られる。

The new type of energy is made from garbage which used to be (　).

(A) deposited　　　(B) discarded　　　(C) disrupted

(5) ....

Unit 12　Language

通訳者の能力とは

A Job for Fast Talkers and Fast Thinkers

　通訳者には、言語の流暢さだけでなく、ある言語で話された内容をスムースに別の言語で表現するための特別な技能が必要とされる。通訳には 2 種類ある。一つは同時通訳、もう一つは逐次通訳である。特に後者には、話されたことを素早く正確にメモを取るという、同時通訳にはない能力が求められる。両者に共通して求められるのは、発話力、集中力、見せ方、話者の意図やニュアンスを感じ取る繊細さなどであるが、最も重要なことは、厳しく訓練して通訳者になることである。

　A career as an interpreter is often attractive to a person with a knack for foreign languages. But it takes more than just fluency in a foreign language to be an interpreter. It is also necessary to cultivate a wide range of special skills related to the task of smoothly expressing the content of a person's spoken comments into another language.

　(　A　) the job of translation, which deals with written texts and allows the translator time to look up words in a dictionary, interpretation requires a person to quickly think of the most appropriate words to convey the content of spoken language.

　There are two basic kinds of interpretation: "simultaneous" or "consecutive."

A Job for Fast Talkers and Fast Thinkers

In the former case, it is necessary to interpret at the same time as a person is talking; whereas in the latter case the interpreter speaks after the other person has finished speaking. Simultaneous interpreting is particularly difficult, (B   ) the interpreter must think quickly, but consecutive interpreting also has its own difficulties, such as the need to quickly jot down accurate notes in order to recall what the speaker said.

Along with learning such skills as note-taking, interpreters need a deep understanding of the specific content of the particular conference or event at which they are interpreting, as well as wide-ranging knowledge in as many other fields as possible. Other obvious abilities that an interpreter needs to develop include public speaking skills, intense concentration, a professional appearance*, and a sensitivity to the meaning, tone, and nuance of spoken words.

Obviously, some people are more suited to* this profession than others. At the very least, a budding interpreter must have a passion for language, a talent for communication, and an insatiable curiosity with regard to knowledge and current events. (C   ) having a pleasing speaking voice is another big plus.

But even with all of those characteristics, it is vital for a person to train diligently to become a professional interpreter. Fortunately, there are numerous interpreting training courses to choose from, including short-term training courses and undergraduate or graduate programs. Such training is crucial for a person to acquire the full range of skills needed to be a competent interpreter, but even more important is the knowledge that is gained through actual work experience. Perhaps someday computer technology will replace the need for actual interpreters, but until that day arrives there will continue to be a need for talented linguists capable of performing this daunting task.　　(406 words)

***appearance**「外見、印象」　***suited to ...** [súːtɪd-]「…するのに適した」発音に注意。

Keywords & Keyphrases

本文に使われている次の語句の意味としてもっとも適切なものを a～l から選びなさい。

1.	(l. 1) knack	a. 在校生、学部の学生	1. ( )
2.	(l. 3) cultivate	b. 才能；技巧	2. ( )
3.	(l. 10) simultaneous	c. 熱心に、勤勉に	3. ( )
4.	(l. 10) consecutive	d. 逐次の、順を追った	4. ( )
5.	(l. 15) jot down	e. 新進気鋭の	5. ( )

UNIT 12   Language

6. (l. 15) recall   f. 同時に行われる［起こる］   6. (   )
7. (l. 24) budding   g. 感じのよい、心地よい   7. (   )
8. (l. 25) insatiable   h. 飽くなき、貪欲な   8. (   )
9. (l. 26) pleasing   i. 大変な、手ごわい   9. (   )
10. (l. 28) diligently   j. をみがく、を修める   10. (   )
11. (l. 30) undergraduate   k. を思い出す   11. (   )
12. (l. 35) daunting   l. を素早くメモする   12. (   )

Exercises

1 本文中の空欄（ A),(B),(C) に入る単語として最も適切なものをそれぞれ①、②の中から選びなさい

(A) ....
(B) ....
(C) ....

(A)	① Like	② Unlike
(B)	① if	② because
(C)	① And	② But

2 質問を読み、正しい答を (A) ～ (D) の中から選びなさい。

Question 1

What is the main purpose of this passage?

(A) To recommend a good job for people who love languages
(B) To offer a basic profile of the job of interpretation
(C) To introduce some of the programs for interpreter training
(D) To compare "simultaneous" and "consecutive" interpretation

Question 2

What is one thing that the passage recommends?

(A) Focusing on "simultaneous interpretation" if possible
(B) Attending conferences to gain wide-ranging knowledge
(C) The importance of proper training to be an interpreter
(D) The fact only a person with a very nice voice could become an interpreter

3 次の英文は本文の内容に関するものである。本文の内容に一致する場合はTを、一致しない場合はFを下線部に記入しなさい。

(A) Anyone who is fluent in a language should be able to interpret. ....

(B) Interpreters tend to prefer "consecutive interpretation" because it is easier.

....

(C) Computer programs will soon replace the need for actual interpreters.

....

4 次は本文の要約文である。空欄（ A ），（ B ），（ C ），（ D ）に下記に与えられたアルファベットで始まる適切な語を入れて完成させなさい。

Having a talent for languages is important for anyone considering a career as an interpreter. But the job also (A) a wide range of other skills, (B) public speaking skills, intense concentration, a professional appearance, and a sensitivity to the meaning, tone, and nuance of spoken words. Even with all of those characteristics, however, it is still (C) for a person to train hard to (D) a professional interpreter.

(A) r......................................

(B) i......................................

(C) i......................................

(D) b......................................

UNIT 12　Language

5　空所に入れる最も適切な語句を選択肢 (A) 〜 (C) から選びなさい。

(1) 私のクラスの先生は，小説を読むことは他者への感情移入を養うことになるとしばしば主張した。

The teacher in my class often argued that reading novels (　　) empathy for others.

　　(A) attracts　　　(B) regulates　　　(C) cultivates

(1) ....

(2) その画用紙でできたリンゴの木は食べられないようではあったが、目には心地よかった。

The construction-paper apple tree didn't look good to eat, but it was (　　) to the eye.

　　(A) sophisticated　　(B) pleasing　　(C) sensitive

(2) ....

(3) 我々の調査によれば、パニックと抑うつが同時に発生することは比較的頻繁に起きる。

According to our research, the (　　) occurrence of panic and depression is relatively frequent.

　　(A) simultaneous　　(B) timely　　(C) contemporary

(3) ....

(4) メグと家族は、彼女が高校を卒業するまで教育を援助するために懸命に働いた。

Meg and her family worked (　　) to support her education until she graduated high school.

　　(A) diligently　　(B) entirely　　(C) reasonably

(4) ....

(5) アメリカ合衆国には 4,000 以上の大学があるので、大学を選ぶことは高校を卒業予定の学生にとって大変な作業だ。

With more than 4,000 universities available in the United States, choosing a university is a (　　) task for the graduating high school student.

　　(A) valid　　(B) sensible　　(C) daunting

(5) ....

Unit 13　Literature

小説はどこに

Graphic Novels

　2005年、TIME誌は、1923年の創刊以来の偉大な小説100冊を発表した。この100冊のリストの中に、特に話題となった1冊があった。コミックブックの一種 *Watchmen* である。1440年の印刷機の発明以来、伝統的な小説が普及しつづけ、絵本は子ども向けというのが伝統的な考えであった。ところが、20世紀に入り映画やアニメが出現し、1930年代までにはコミックは軽いエンターテインメントとして人気を得たのである。*Watchmen* はこうした流れの嚆矢と言える。

　In 2005, Time Magazine* created a stir upon publishing a list of the 100 greatest English language novels since 1923, the year the magazine was founded. While any such list is subjective and therefore controversial, this time the larger buzz came from one entry that was not a novel in the traditional sense. Making the list was "Watchmen,"* a graphic novel — or picture novel — first serialized and later published in book form in 1987. The high regard for "Watchmen" hints that the concept of what comprises a novel is changing and that combining words with art may one day play a bigger part in the future of literature.

　Mankind has always told stories through pictures. This can be seen by ancient cave drawings found in different countries in the world. Yet such a story

UNIT 13　Literature

form has been historically difficult to mass-produce. The development of the written word and the invention of the printing press in 1440 led naturally to the (　　A　　) of the traditional novel. Picture books were considered more for children. Yet, in the 20th century, the advent of motion pictures and animation began to change this thinking. By the 1930s comic books were booming. While these were often considered light entertainment, a trend toward longer and more serious comics finally led to graphic novels, of which "Watchmen" was one of the first.

　　"Watchmen"—written by Alan Moore and drawn by Dave Gibbons—tells the story of a team of aging superheroes who live in retirement in a society that no longer needs such heroes. Now, some unknown villain may be scheming to murder them off. The story balances mystery and science fiction with social commentary. The novel was (　　B　　) and was eventually released as a feature film* in 2009.

　　While such graphic novels have long been well-regarded in Japan, where they are known as manga, "Watchmen" and other works like it helped spur the western market. Now annual sales for both graphic novels and comic books are approaching the one billion dollar mark. The advance of the Internet and the video game industry has also helped blend art with words. In fact, younger generations may be far (　　C　　) inclined to pick up a graphic novel or view one online than read the large blocks of print of traditional books. The colorful pictures and fast pace seems to better match the briefer attention span of modern man.

　　The age of the graphic novel may be upon us. "Watchmen" is a proud pioneer of a coming day when lists of fine books may be filled with such works.

(432 words)

***Time Magazine**　アメリカの雑誌『タイム』のこと。　*"**Watchmen**"　全12巻のアメリカンコミックの大作。映画化もされた。　*feature film　「長編映画」

Keywords & Keyphrases

本文に使われている次の語句の意味としてもっとも適切なものを a~l から選びなさい。

1. (l. 1) stir　　　　　　　a. 騒動、混乱　　　　　　1. (　　)
2. (l. 3) subjective　　　　b. 意見、主張；説明　　　2. (　　)
3. (l. 3) controversial　　 c. 騒音；興奮　　　　　　3. (　　)
4. (l. 4) buzz　　　　　　 d. 悪党、悪者；悪役　　　4. (　　)
5. (l. 5) serialize　　　　　e. 出現、到来　　　　　　5. (　　)

Graphic Novels

6. (l. 6) hint
7. (l. 7) comprise
8. (l. 14) advent
9. (l. 21) villain
10. (l. 21) scheme
11. (l. 23) commentary
12. (l. 26) spur

f. を刺激する、を促進させる
g. を暗示する、を示唆する
h. を構成する；〜から成る
i. をたくらむ、の計画を立てる
j. を連載する、を放送する
k. 主観的な、感覚的な
l. 議論を引き起こす［招く］

6. (　　)
7. (　　)
8. (　　)
9. (　　)
10. (　　)
11. (　　)
12. (　　)

Exercises

1 本文中の空欄（ A ），（ B ），（ C ）に入る単語として最も適切なものをそれぞれ①、②の中から選びなさい。

(A) ....
(B) ....
(C) ....

(A)　① expansion　　② decrease
(B)　① well-received　② refused
(C)　① more　　　　② less

2 質問を読み、正しい答を (A)〜(D) の中から選びなさい。

Question 1

What is the main thrust of this passage?

(A) "Watchmen" made Time Magazine's 2005 list of the top 100 English Language novels.
(B) "Watchmen" is indicative of a new direction in literature, the graphic novel.
(C) "Watchmen" and other graphic novels are now reaching near the one billion dollar mark in annual sales.
(D) "Watchmen" and other graphic novels are highly acclaimed for their combination of words with art.

Question 2

According to this passage, what technology influenced the birth of graphic novels?

(A) The invention of the printing press
(B) The advance of the Internet
(C) The founding of Time Magazine
(D) The dawn of motion pictures and animation

63

UNIT 13 Literature

3 次の英文は本文の内容に関するものである。本文の内容に一致する場合はTを、一致しない場合はFを下線部に記入しなさい。

(A) Younger readers may be more interested in graphic novels than traditional ones. ....

(B) The plot of "Watchman" involves the founding of a team of superheroes. ....

(C) Graphic novels are considered more serious than comic books. ....

4 次は本文の要約文である。空欄（ A ）〜（ E ）に下記に与えられたアルファベットで始まる適切な1-2語を入れて完成させなさい。

The popularity of graphic novels is growing, as can be seen by Time Magazine's inclusion of "Watchmen" in the top 100 English language novels in 2005. While people have always been interested in telling stories through art, picture books were long considered mostly for children. (A) and (B) gradually changed this view and lightly-regarded comic books slowly evolved into more serious works of art. This trend in literature has been further promoted by the expansion of the (C) and (D), which also combined (E) with pictures.

(A) M............................ p............................

(B) a............................

(C) I............................

(D) v............................ g............................

(E) w............................

Graphic Novels

5 空所に入れる最も適切な語句を選択肢 (A) ～ (C) から選びなさい。

(1) 植物が感情を持っているという考えは、まだ多くの科学者のあいだで議論の的となっている。

The idea that plants feel emotions remains (　　) among many scientists.

   (A) probable　　　(B) controversial　　(C) reasonable

(1) ....

(2) その会議は日本の全県からの代表者で構成されるのだが、10月31日、大阪で開催された。

The Conference, which (　　) representatives from all the Japanese prefectures, assembled at Osaka on 31st October.

   (A) comprised　　(B) confined　　　(C) imposed

(2) ....

(3) この解説と分析が貴社のビジネスに関係している場合、本サイトへ登録することをご検討ください。

If this (　　) and analysis is relevant to your business, please consider registering on this site.

   (A) commentary　　(B) prospect　　　(C) retreat

(3) ....

(4) 新しいプロジェクトに対する私の考えは主観的すぎるのでうまくいかない、とダンは言った。

Dan suggested an idea I had for the new project wouldn't work because it would be too (　　).

   (A) decisive　　　(B) positive　　　(C) subjective

(4) ....

(5) この科目は、知的障害を抱える子どもに対する教育の充実をはかることのできる教育者を訓練することを意図している。

This major is (　　) to train educators who can help enrich education for children with intellectual disabilities.

   (A) schemed　　　(B) integrated　　(C) asserted

(5) ....

Unit 14 Culture

アムステルダム風景

Canal Houses

アムステルダムには運河が張り巡らされ、運河沿いには canal house と呼ばれる美しい家並みが連なっている。この運河は 17 世紀初頭から作られ始めた。当時、オランダは貿易や投資で世界をリードしていたため、運河沿いには豪華な家が並び始めた。だが、元々、土地が狭く高価だったため、それぞれの家は高く細長い形となった。また、低地ゆえ洪水が多かったため大切なものは上の階に収納された。品物はもっぱら家の外壁づたいに引き上げたという。

　The Dutch city of Amsterdam is webbed by a system of canals not unlike city thoroughfares. Along those canals stand long lines of unusual homes known as "canal houses." These canal houses are an important part of Amsterdam culture and today serve as both tourist attractions and reminders of the wealthy history of the city.

　Amsterdam's largest canals were built in the early 17th century, as part of residential planning. In those days, Holland was the world's leading nation in terms of trade and investment. Amsterdam was growing rapidly and the canals were designed to help the city expand in an orderly manner. Soon the canals were lined with the extravagant homes that we still see today.

(A) the original plots of land were small and expensive, all canal houses tend to be tall and narrow. In front, these houses stand shoulder-to-shoulder and open directly to the sidewalk. Due to frequent flooding, many homes have steep stairways leading to a front door set high above the walkway. As signs of the wealth of the times in which they were built*, canal houses also have tall windows and pointed gables*. The differences in heights and colors of each home add a checkered* quality to the view of each canal. Behind many homes also lie quaint and fashionable gardens.

Because of the flooding, canal house residents took to storing important goods on their upper floors. Yet, the narrow nature of the houses made it impossible to carry large items up the slender staircases. (B), each canal house sports a metal hook from its central gable. When moving furniture or other similar goods, residents attach a rope and pulley to this hook and raise the items on the exterior. To make this more convenient, each home was constructed with a slight forward lean. This lean helps prevent raised items from brushing against the walls of the house. (C), to many observers this forward lean seems precarious. Although perfectly safe, some canal houses almost appear ready to topple forward onto passersby!

Since 2010 the canals of Amsterdam have been listed as a World Heritage Site. Travelers to the city all enjoy viewing the lovely canals and tour boats depart every few minutes. Yet, the beauty of the canals is further enhanced by the lengthy rows of attractive canal houses, which are still used today by the active residents of Amsterdam.   (396 words)

*the times in which they were built 「それらがつくりつけられた時代」build in 「(家具などを)つくりつけにする、組みこむ」 *gable 「切り妻、破風（ひさしの下の三角形の部分）」 *checkered 「格子模様の」

Keywords & Keyphrases

本文に使われている次の語句の意味としてもっとも適切なものを a~l から選びなさい。

1. (l. 1) web   a. 幹線道路、道路   1. (　)
2. (l. 1) not unlike   b. 小区画の土地   2. (　)
3. (l. 2) thoroughfare c. 滑車   3. (　)
4. (l. 10) extravagant d. ～をクモの巣のように覆う   4. (　)
5. (l. 11) plot   e. ～にこする、～にかする   5. (　)

UNIT 14 Culture

6. (l. 18) quaint f. ～を設置する、～を付ける 6. ( )
7. (l. 19) take to g. 倒れる、ぐらつく 7. ( )
8. (l. 22) sport h. ～が習慣になる 8. ( )
9. (l. 23) pulley i. ～と同じで、～と違わない 9. ( )
10. (ll. 25-) brush against j. 古風で魅力的な；風変わりな 10. ( )
11. (l. 27) precarious k. 不安定な、危険な 11. ( )
12. (l. 28) topple l. ぜいたくな、豪華な 12. ( )

Exercises

1 本文中の空欄（ A),(B),(C) に入る単語として最も適切なものをそれぞれ①、②の中から選びなさい。

(A) ....
(B) ....
(C) ....

(A) ① Because   ② Although
(B) ① Thus   ② However
(C) ① Fortunately ② Yet

2 質問を読み、正しい答を (A)～(D) の中から選びなさい。

Question 1

What is the main focus of this passage?

(A) The development and usage of Amsterdam's famous canals
(B) The unique features of houses along Amsterdam's canals
(C) How Amsterdam's canal houses first came to be constructed
(D) How Amsterdam expanded orderly in the early 17th century

Question 2

According to the passage, which of the following is NOT a feature of canal houses?

(A) A variety of colors
(B) Narrow structures with differences in height
(C) Spacious staircases that reach to the upper floors
(D) High windows with front doors set far up from the sidewalk

Canal Houses

3 次の英文は本文の内容に関するものである。本文の内容に一致する場合はTを、一致しない場合はFを下線部に記入しなさい。

(A) The canal system of Amsterdam has been a World Heritage site for about 400 years. ....

(B) The metal hooks at the top of each canal house are for lifting furniture. ....

(C) Canal houses sometimes fall forward due to their lean. ....

4 次は本文の要約文である。空欄（ A ）～（ I ）に入る適切な語を①～⑫から選び完成させなさい。同じ語を複数回使うこともある。なお、文頭に入る単語も小文字で表記している。

In the early 17th century Amsterdam designed a system of canals to help with city expansion. (A) and (B) homes came to be built along these canals, homes now known as "canal houses." Canal houses have various unique features, such as their (C) size, (D) windows and (E) gables. The (F) size makes it (G) to move items to the (H) floors. At the same time, (I) floor storage has been historically important due to flooding. Nowadays, canal houses add to the beauty of the city of Amsterdam.

(A) .... (B) ....
(C) .... (D) ....
(E) .... (F) ....
(G) .... (H) ....
(I) ....

① short	② tall
③ narrow	④ wide
⑤ small	⑥ large
⑦ low	⑧ high
⑨ lower	⑩ upper
⑪ easy	⑫ difficult

UNIT 14　Culture

5　空所に入れる最も適切な語句を選択肢 (A) 〜 (C) から選びなさい。

(1) 王子に敬意を表して催された晩餐会は、とても豪華ですばらしかった。

The banquet organized in honor of the prince was so (　　) and magnificent.

　(A) extreme　　　(B) extravagant　　　(C) elaborate

(1) ....

(2) 妊娠しているとき、毎日よく新鮮な牛乳を熱心に飲んだものだ。

When I was expectant, I used to (　　) drinking fresh cow's milk daily.

　(A) take to　　　(B) get in　　　(C) put on

(2) ....

(3) 最近、その独裁者の政権は倒れ、彼は監獄に放り込まれた。

Recently, the dictator's regime (　　) down and he was thrown into jail.

　(A) toppled　　　(B) pulled　　　(C) slowed

(3) ....

(4) ハリーがドアを開けると、突然何かが彼の足にさっとふれた。

As Harry opened the door, something suddenly (　　) against his leg.

　(A) stood　　　(B) appealed　　　(C) brushed

(4) ....

(5) このエリアは、ホテルに歩いて行ける距離に多くの古風で魅力的なショップとレストランがあるのが特徴だ。

This area features many (　　) shops and restaurants within walking distance of the hotel.

　(A) exotic　　　(B) quaint　　　(C) outstanding

(5) ....

Unit 15　Sociology

運転中になぜキレる？

Road Rage

Road rage（運転中にキレること）ということばは、1980年代後半にロサンジェルスの高速道路における無謀運転を指したが、後に全米に広がった。背景にある要素としては、急ぐ気持・車の高性能化・道路の高速化などがあるが、渋滞や急な割り込み、クラクションなどに対するイライラが road rage につながる。また、運転席という閉じられた空間にいるために他者への抑制がはずれることも原因の一つと考えられている。

　"Road rage" is a term that was first created to describe aggressive driving on the congested freeways* of Los Angeles in the late 1980s, but the actual phenomenon is certainly older and not limited to Los Angeles or even the United States. Countries around the world now report incidents of reckless driving seemingly fueled by a sense of anger or impatience. Such road rage can lead to accidents and, in worse cases, even cause fatalities. One key to limiting these incidents is to understand the causes behind road rage.

　At first glance, the cause might seem obvious. Many drivers are in a hurry and the power of their automobiles and the openness of the road are emblematic of what they expect: a quick journey to their destination. The word "freeway"

UNIT 15 Sociology

itself expresses a lack of obstruction or restriction. Yet, traffic is not always smooth. The abundance of cars necessitates slower movement, often made worse by road construction or accidents. (　　A　　), some drivers feel frustrated and take chances to speed ahead. They might cut off* other cars or slide abruptly between lanes. Other drivers might then react back with shouts, gestures or loud blasts of their horns. They might even compete to stay ahead. Thus road rage is born.

Another cause is the isolated environment of the driver. Drivers operate both inside and outside of society. When in traffic they are of course within the flow of a larger group and need to relate orderly to other autos. But at the same time each driver is alone in his or her car and may feel free and uninhibited. They may show (　　B　　) hesitance in voicing their opinions in regards to other drivers, confident that no one will hear them. But this emotion can often translate into sudden and aggressive behavior behind the wheel. With road rage, private feelings can soon become public actions.

A final cause lies in the dynamic nature of automobiles themselves. Fast and powerful, they lend each driver a sense of strength and security*. Drivers may feel invulnerable within the metallic safety of their vehicles. They may see themselves as having the speed and control to circumvent any difficulty. They may thus (　　C　　) chances where normally they would not. They may also react to other cars in a combative manner.

Three words can remove the "rage" from road rage: "Take it easy." Drivers have to slow down and realize an automobile must not become an extension for their emotions. Being polite is important, maybe especially so when driving a car.

(422 words)

*freeway　日本でいう「高速道路」のこと。　*cut off「（通路などを）さえぎる」　*lend...security　lend A B「AにBを与える」

Keywords & Keypharases

本文に使われている次の語句の意味としてもっとも適切なものを a~l から選びなさい。

1. (l. 1) rage　　　　　　a. （事故・戦争などによる）死者　　　1. (　　)
2. (l. 4) reckless　　　　b. 大音響；爆発　　　　　　　　　　　2. (　　)
3. (l. 5) impatience　　　c. 躊躇、ためらい　　　　　　　　　　3. (　　)
4. (l. 6) fatalities　　　　d. 短気、イライラ　　　　　　　　　　4. (　　)

72

5.	(l. 9) emblematic	e. 激怒；猛威	5. ( )
6.	(l. 12) necessitate	f. を余儀なくさせる、を要する	6. ( )
7.	(l. 16) blast	g. を回避する、を避ける	7. ( )
8.	(l. 21) uninhibited	h. 不死身の、傷つけられない	8. ( )
9.	(l. 22) hesitance	i. 象徴した、象徴の	9. ( )
10.	(l. 28) invulnerable	j. 無謀な、無茶な	10. ( )
11.	(l. 29) circumvent	k. 闘争的な、好戦的な	11. ( )
12.	(l. 31) combative	l. 遠慮のない、抑制されない	12. ( )

Exercises

1 本文中の空欄（ A ），（ B ），（ C ）に入る単語として最も適切なものをそれぞれ①、②の中から選びなさい。

(A) ....
(B) ....
(C) ....

(A) ① Hence   ② However
(B) ① much   ② no
(C) ① take   ② lose

2 質問を読み、正しい答を (A)～(D) の中から選びなさい。

Question 1

What is the main idea of this passage?

(A) Drivers should strive to be polite in any situation.
(B) The occurrence known as "road rage" has several causes.
(C) Aggressive driving has spread from Los Angeles around the world.
(D) Road rage can lead to accidents and even fatalities.

Question 2

Why might drivers express themselves freely when within their car?

(A) They have no need to relate to other automobiles.
(B) That is part of the meaning of the word, "freeway."
(C) Drivers should show confidence when they drive.
(D) They may feel sure no one else can hear them.

UNIT 15   Sociology

3 次の英文は本文の内容に関するものである。本文の内容に一致する場合はTを、一致しない場合はFを下線部に記入しなさい。

(A) "Road rage" first began on the freeways of Los Angeles.　　　　..................

(B) Traffic frustration often relates to road rage.　　　　..................

(C) The speed and power of cars can encourage drivers to commit risky behavior.

....

4 次は本文の要約文である。空欄（ A ）〜（ E ）に下記に与えられたアルファベットで始まる適切な語を入れて完成させなさい。

Road rage is a name given to aggressive and impatient driving. This reckless driving may be (A) by feelings of frustration when (B) is not moving well. Drivers may also react with too much (C), thinking themselves removed from the eyes and ears of others. The security of an automobile may also spur drivers toward sudden aggression. To limit road rage, (D) need to relax and try to be more (E).

(A) c..................................

(B) t..................................

(C) e..................................

(D) d..................................

(E) p..................................

Road Rage

5 空所に入れる最も適切な語句を選択肢 (A) 〜 (C) から選びなさい。

(1) ジョニーは自分をバカにしたと友だちをなじっていたとき、かっとなって我を忘れてしまった。

John lost control of himself in a fit of (　　) while accusing his friend of cheating on him.

　(A) threat　　　　(B) conflict　　　　(C) rage

(1) ....

(2) 大音響を聞いて、ダニエルは何が起きているのか見るために外に走り出た。

Hearing the (　　), Daniel ran outside to see what was going on.

　(A) blast　　　　(B) disaster　　　　(C) issue

(2) ....

(3) そのクライアントは急にイライラして、注文をキャンセルすることに決めた。

The client suddenly showed (　　) and decided to cancel the order.

　(A) impatience　　(B) discourage　　(C) depression

(3) ....

(4) 死者もなく、負傷者もほとんどいなかったが、赤十字は仮設のシェルターを提供することで忙しかった。

There were no (　　) and few injuries, however the Red Cross was busy providing temporary shelters.

　(A) critics　　　　(B) fatalities　　　　(C) defects

(4) ....

(5) 私の望みは、すべての人があらゆる病気や身体的な不全に対して無敵になり、それが続くことだ。

My wish is that all people become and remain (　　) to any sort of disease and bodily malfunction.

　(A) invulnerable　(B) inevitable　(C) indispensable

(5) ....

Comprehension Reading:
Getting Key Skills through 15 Topics
読解力を磨く現代の話題15章

編著者 　トム・ディロン
　　　　　マイケル・シャワティ
　　　　　西　谷　恒　志
発行者 　山　口　隆　史

発　行　所 　　㈱ 音羽書房鶴見書店
〒113-0033　東京都文京区本郷 3-26-13
　　　　　　　　　TEL 03-3814-0491
　　　　　　　　　FAX 03-3814-9250
URL: https://www.otowatsurumi.com
e-mail: info@otowatsurumi.com

2017 年 3 月 　1 日　　初版発行
2024 年 3 月 15 日　　4 刷発行

組版・装幀　ほんのしろ
印刷・製本　（株）シナノ パブリッシング プレス
■ 落丁・乱丁本はお取り替えいたします。

EC-064